Joe Stahlkuppe

Basset
Hounds

Everything About Purchase,
Feeding, and Health Care

BARRON'S

2 CONTENTS

DOGS DOGS DO

UNDERSTANDING THE BASSET HOUND

Long and low with one of the most appealing faces in dogdom, the Basset Hound can be both a joy and a challenge. Taking time to get to know this laid-back hound will not only be useful for a prospective owner, but necessary for the happiness of the dog and the human.

The Basset Hound is one of the most recognizable dog breeds in the world. From a short-legged French hunting hound, the Basset has become a sad-faced Renaissance Dog. Transformed by television into a star, a corporate logo, and a regular media darling, this long-bodied, laid-back hound has millions of fans who know the breed only by its appearance.

Originally bred to be a solid, slow-moving, pack dog, the Basset is much more than "just another pretty face." The breed continues to win in the dog show ring. Some Bassets are quite able obedience trial dogs. An increasing number of Basset Hounds are returning to the

The Basset Hound combines humor and hound in an appealing low-slung, hangdog package that never fails to bring a smile.

field as rabbit hounds or in the growing sport of Basset field trialing.

Media star, best-in-show winner, magazine coverdog, the Basset has come a long way from being a low-slung French rabbit dog. A master of subtle, sleepy charm, the Basset has taken relaxation to new heights. Calm and imperturbable, the Basset has taken its success in low, slow stride and still maintains a well-deserved reputation as an excellent family pet.

Origin and History of the Basset Hound

Over the centuries, the French have developed many types of hunting dogs, especially hunting hounds. There may have been as many as a dozen varieties of these hounds that had

very short legs, identified as *bas* or "low"
hounds. Bred to work thick cover and heavy
woods, these low-set hounds did not need the
blazing speed of a Greyhound, the size and
fighting ability of the Wolfhound, the agility of
the Foxhound, or even the merry quickness of
the Beagle. The Basset Hound depended on
excellent scenting abilities, dogged persever-
ance, and endurance.

At a time when most hunters used primitive
weapons such as spears, nets, and clubs, the
slowness of the Basset was a definite asset.
Hunters could easily keep pace with the Basset,
depending on the sensitive nose of the short
hound to pick up and stay with scents other,
speedier, hounds would run right by.

The sense of smell of the Basset Hound rivals
that of its near kin and taller cousin, the Bloodhound. The Basset, except for its very short legs,
is closer in type and personality to the Bloodhound than it is to most of the other scent-
hound breeds. Both share many of the same
abilities and some of the same problems.

Saint Hubert Hounds

Both the Bloodhound and the Basset Hound
are thought to be descendants of the legendary
Saint Hubert hounds. Saint Hubert, a churchman
who became the patron saint of hunting, was
supposedly a hunter and hunting dog fancier
held in wide regard. During the sixth century he
developed packs of hounds that were held in
high esteem. After Hubert's death, the monks of
his abbey continued to breed these hounds and
often presented them to royalty.

Other Origins

Other origins for the Basset Hound include the
probability of a genetic mutation for short legs
that was found useful and that firmly established itself. Some authorities tied the Basset
Hound and the Dachshund together in a plausi-
ble scenario where the two short-legged hunting
breeds stemmed from common, low-slung fore-
bears but took on different hunting roles,
markedly different personalities, and a different
appearance other than sharing a low height.

The exact ancient origins of the Basset will
probably remain unknown, but the more modern history of the breed involves several dedicated French dog breeders, many equally
dedicated British supporters, and some American enthusiasts. This multinational approach
ultimately brought this low-set, sad-faced,

*The Basset comes from a long history of
hunting hounds for several types of game.*

As a trailing or scent hound, the Basset is quite capable of following his nose away from home. When alone outside, the Basset should always be securely fenced in a kennel or backyard.

plodding hunting hound to a position of popularity throughout the world.

French Contributors

In France, the Comte le Couteulx de Canteleu, M. Louis Lane, M. Masson, the Marquis de Tournon, M. Leon Verrier, and others were pivotal contributors to the development, standardization, and improvement of the Basset Hound. Starting with the divergent gene pool of short French hunting dogs, these key breeders each had somewhat different ideas about what they wanted in Basset Hounds. Each, however, worked diligently to produce Basset Hounds of overall quality. Finally, a blending of these different strains (or families) of hounds gave an

equally dedicated cadre of English breeders the foundation for what would become the modern Basset Hound.

English Breeders

In the late nineteenth century and early twentieth century, significant English fans of the Basset Hound were Lords Galway and Onslow, the Prince and Princess of Wales, and Queen Alexandra. Perhaps the most important English breeder was Sir Everett Millais. Sir Everett studied the best of the French hounds, conducted a myriad of breeding and crossbreeding experiments, imported the best of French Bassets, and thoroughly championed the breed. It was through his efforts that the Basset

Bassets are the quintessential pack dogs. Stemming from their long hunting heritage, they usually get along well with other dogs.

Hound attracted the attention of English dog breeding society, and subsequently, American dog breeders.

North America

Short-legged French hounds of the *bas* sort had been brought to North America for more than 100 years before 1885 when the first Basset Hound was registered with the American Kennel Club. Sources suggest that George Washington received some of these short hounds, referred to by some sources as "bench-legged beagles," from the Marquis de Lafayette. Many other dog breeders and sporting dog enthusiasts brought earlier versions of the sturdy Basset to the United States. There were many Americans who brought dogs directly from France; others favored British importations. Some American dog fanciers turned to both sources for the best available Bassets. One of the most significant of these American Bas-

set fans was Gerald Livingston, who became informally known as the "father of the American Basset Hound." Livingston did much to bring the French hound, which was improved by the British, to the attention and then to the kennels of the American dog-owning public. His influence is still felt in the breed today as is the influence of great dogs that he produced.

In 1935 the Basset Hound Club of America was founded and in 1937 this organization was accepted as the official breed club by the American Kennel Club. This recognition was all the Basset Hound needed to begin its ascent up the ranks of popular breeds.

The Personality of the Basset Hound

The Basset Hound is a paradox in the personality department. In many ways these short hounds have such sad-eyed charm that it is

BASSET ASSET
Bassets need a solid, loving,
and consistent lifestyle.

hard to imagine that they can also be stubborn and independent. The Basset can be the best of pets, but it needs good, consistent training and discipline. People who want to add a Basset to their family should become knowledgeable about the breed to provide the best kind of home for this usually calm—except when on a hot scent—breed.

As with many breeds that have achieved a high degree of public acceptance, recognition, and popularity, the Basset Hound is sometimes perceived as more plaything than pet. Bassets and potential Basset owners deserve a more realistic and humane fate. Bassets are short but not small dogs. They are breathing, living creatures, not plush stuffed animals to be brought out to elicit oohs and ahhs from friends and neighbors.

Bassets are adorable as puppies and appealing as adults. They are among the most photogenic of all dogs during all stages of their lives. They are, however, still dogs and need the things most dogs need. They will want the things most dogs want. They will make the mistakes that most dogs do. Humans who want a really good dog as a pet can often find just what they want in the Basset. People who want some canine conversation piece should save themselves, and an innocent dog, the trouble!

The Basset Hound can be very good as a family pet, in the field, in the show ring, in obedience work, *if* it wants to be! The task for any Basset owner is to encourage, develop, and help the Basset in doing the right things! Unfortu-

nately, some owners fall for that hangdog expression, that long and low body, the stubby legs, and see the Basset Hound as something too cute to control, or too appealing to discipline. This is an error of large proportions and can hurt an otherwise excellent dog.

The Basset Hound as a Companion and Family Pet

The Basset Hound can be a great companion animal. Usually sweet and loving, the Basset seems to fit very well with its human owners. Slow and deliberate most of the time, the Basset Hound is not a dog for the hyperactive owner. The Basset goes along best at its own pace and in activities that fit its demeanor and physical stature. A thoughtful individual or family considering a Basset should always keep this in mind. The person who wants to challenge for the national championship in Frisbee-catching should pick another breed than the Basset!

Bassets are loving companions for humans at all ages. Perhaps a part of their pack hound heritage, the Basset can develop a special, individualized bond with each person in a family. Bassets are sturdy enough for play with supervised children. They are certainly calm enough to spend a quiet day at home. Bassets can more than hold their own as hunting and tracking dogs. Bassets from show dog backgrounds can be excellent in the show ring. While maybe not the dog for everyone, the Basset Hound can fill the need for many people seeking an affectionate, attractive, super-calm family pet.

Protecting Your Basset
Each family member needs to take special care of this special pet.

✔ The Basset can be injured if a small child perceives the dog as a long, short pony and tries to ride it. Basset backs are not designed for such stresses.

✔ Older children can leave doors or gates open and a nose-following Basset can trail its way away from home. Its poor sense of direction prevents the dog from back-tracking itself and returning. Often so intent on following a delicious-smelling scent, a loose Basset will follow the track right into a roadway and tragedy.

✔ Young Bassets, with their abnormally long bodies and heavily built fronts and chests need to be kept off the couch, off the bed, off even low walls. Built like a train, this low-to-the-ground canine is not meant for jumping and hurdling. Many broken bones, strains, and other preventable injuries can be avoided by keeping the Basset out of harm's way.

✔ Eyes and ears of the Basset are both droopy and right at a level where some potentially dangerous injury-maker can hurt them. A Basset's family must take responsibility for this slow, lovable pet that may not recognize the things that can hurt it.

✔ Bassets like to eat, sometimes don't get enough exercise, and are thus subject to obesity than can shorten their lives and bring on some painful physical problems. They can be subject, as are other deep-chested dogs, to gastric torsion (or bloat) cases.

✔ Their deeply wrinkled facial skin requires some special care and cleaning. Water is inviting, but swimming is difficult for the Basset that could tumble into the family pool and drown.

Rest

One dog show judge referred to the calm demeanor of the Basset as "rather like the first stages of a coma, slow motion, or sleepwalking." Bassets do like their beauty rest. Low activity levels make them the opposite of some terriers and other breeds that are almost in perpetual motion. Bassets do run and have a good time, but they do it in their own way. Their own way can sometimes seem like the Basset is being stubborn. A patient, but persistent, dog owner can win out because the Basset is also usually not demanding or aggressive.

House-training

The Basset can take a little longer to become house-trained. (See House-training, page 49.) Patience and persistence are also needed here. The family that really wants a Basset as a pet can help the youngster learn this valuable lesson. This excellent family pet needs just a little more encouragement and support to understand when and where it needs to go to relieve itself.

Bassets, even with their shortcomings, can be among the gentlest, most loving of pets. Their calm dispositions make them an excellent pet for the right pet owner. When a thoroughly prepared dog owner finds the right Basset, and gives it the right care, the result can be one of the best of dog-human companion relationships!

The Basset Hound in the Show Ring

The Basset Hound may seem homely to some people, but this short hound has many admirers among the dog show crowd. While maintaining its capacity to be a good pet, and an able sporting dog, the Basset has also firmly established itself in the highly competitive world of conformation dog shows. This short, but charis-

Not as hyper as many of the terrier breeds, the Basset nevertheless has a charm and charisma all its own. This lovely, black-saddled female shows the reflective side of her personality.

matic hound is always a favorite with the crowds that visit dog shows.

Veteran dog breeders and handlers tell of an interesting metamorphosis that seems to come over many a sleepy-appearing Basset when it is time to enter exhibition competition. A show-quality Basset, which may have slept for hours in apparently relaxed boredom before time to enter the show ring, will often become showy (in a Basset sort of way), projecting a winsome and winning image to the dog show judge and to all other onlookers. Other Bassets have to be awakened to go to the show ring and seem more concerned in getting the judging over so they can finish their naps.

Quality exhibition Bassets come from quality exhibition stock. They are usually groomed, trained, and prepared for a show career if they are to achieve greatness in the show ring. Aided by the variety of attractive Basset Hound colors and markings, these dogs win their share of top awards.

The Basset Hound and Obedience Trial Work

While the hound group as a rule is sometimes overshadowed in obedience trials by other breed classifications, there are some hounds represented there. The Basset is no exception. While some Bassets are more difficult to train than others, the breed can certainly be successful in obedience work.

Experienced dog trainers and novices alike have campaigned their low-slung students to highly prized titles. Not as numerous in these activities (few hound breeds are), Bassets have won several titles and do very well in aspects of obedience that emphasize trailing, tracking, and scenting abilities.

Bassets have a laid-back personality, but a definite joy of living.

Obedience trial dogs are often one-person dogs. They need to please one human over all others. This bond is helpful in training, but it can lead to an exclusivity that keeps some obedience dogs from interacting as successfully with strangers and other family members. None of this is a problem for the Basset. Bassets love everybody. Their noses also serve as distraction providers. A pleasing scent can take some Bassets' minds right off the task at hand.

The Pluses and Problems of Popularity

Bassets suffer from popularity like many other breeds. Informed advocates of most breeds dread, rather than embrace, great popularity for their favorite varieties. They have learned that when a breed becomes popular, its overall quality may decline.

The photogenic Basset has become internationally well known. A popular television show from the 1950's, "The People's Choice," starring former child star Jackie Cooper, featured Cleo, a red and white female Basset. Cleo's character was also "heard" in a voice-over and often had the show's best lines. Cleo became an instant success and increased Basset popularity.

Another early TV Basset was "Pokey" who shared the small screen with no less a canine legend than Lassie, him/herself. Pokey belonged to Lassie's young owner's best friend. Still another Basset to achieve widespread recognition was the Basset logo for a popular brand of leisure shoes. Perhaps chosen as an image for this product to accent relaxation, the Basset has served as the major marketing tool for these shoes for decades.

Popularity for a dog breed always has its price. When a breed is relatively unknown to the general public, it is usually bred by experienced, knowledgeable fans who strive for a high level of quality. When a breed achieves wide popularity, inexperienced people allow dogs of lesser quality to reproduce because popularity always guarantees a quick-sale market for the resulting puppies. That some of these puppies may have behavioral or physical defects, or genetically transmitted problems, doesn't seem to occur to, or matter to, some of these people.

Ultimately, a popular breed will suffer as more and more poor-quality specimens are pro-

---

BASSET ASSET

Basset ownership should never be a spur-of-the moment decision. A good Basset home is a prepared Basset home.

---

duced. Bad behavior or health problems fueled by poor breeding practices become part of the public's conception of how popular this or that breed is, whether it is true or not. Many dog people say that the greater the popularity of the breed, the more careful should the search be for a dog or puppy of that breed.

The Basset Personality Summary

There are a number of canine personality indicators that can give a reasonably accurate overview of Bassets as a breed:

Overall Activity Level: The Basset is often quite low in overall activity;

Barking: The Basset is not silent, but neither is the breed excessively noisy. This also makes the Basset less effective in barking at intruders;

Territoriality: Bassets, as would be natural for a pack hound breed, are not very concerned about their "turf" rights. Aggressive behavior by a Basset toward other dogs is still well below such behavior, on average, of all dog breeds. Male Bassets do show such aggressiveness more than do females.

Human Interaction: Bassets aren't likely to bite small children, nor are they likely to try to gain control over the humans in the household. Though very sweet and loving dogs, Bassets don't need the constant pats of reassurance from their owners that some breeds require.

Trainability: Bassets aren't top obedience

scholars. Some Bassets do well enough in obedience training to win titles. Basset males are not quite as easy to house-train as females.

Behavior: Bassets enjoy their own level of participation in play. Don't expect the average Basset to frisk and frolic in the same manner one would expect from the more active terrier breeds.

Bassets also are not as likely to engage in destructive behaviors as much as many breeds.

Before any pet is brought into a home, all members of that home should be carefully coached about what is appropriate and kind treatment of a youngster.

LIVING WITH A BASSET HOUND

Choosing to live with a Basset Hound is different from many other breeds. Bassets are both delightful and very companionable, if they are accepted as what they are and not judged on a scale gauged on the behavior of other kinds of dogs. Slower and less demonstrative than sprightly terriers and the like, Bassets have a mellowness that brings them many fans.

Sharing your life with a Basset Hound is an enjoyable experience made even more so if you understand the uniqueness of the breed. Trying to mold the calm and docile Basset into another type of dog will be a mistake. Let the Basset Hound be just what it is and you will usually be very pleased with the result.

Not Tall, But Not Small

The Basset Hound is not a small dog, it is a large dog with short legs. Males can routinely weigh 50 pounds (23 kg) or more while stand-

Possessing a humble (some say clownish) nobility, Basset Hounds, after the Beagle, are among the most popular scent hounds in the world.

ing only 14 inches (35 cm) high at the shoulder. The Basset packs a lot of dog into a long, low-slung package. This fairly uncommon canine form brings with it some special considerations.

The Basset Hound lives life down where many potential indoor and outdoor dangers exist: sharp corners, briars, protruding wires, and dozens of others. Many hazards are right at Basset-eye level or lower where they could damage the underside of the dog.

Basset Hounds as House Pets

The Basset is not built to be a lap dog. The average person might even have difficulty picking up an adult Basset and some handling, if done incorrectly, could injure this long-bodied dog. Young Bassets should *never* be

allowed to go up or down stairs. Stairs can put great physical stress on their still-developing front legs and chest.

Bassets can do well living inside or outside. Males need more patience to become house-trained than do females, but a persistent owner can handle this training task. The Basset fits in well with most families. Families with swimming pools need to be aware that some Bassets don't swim well and can become disoriented about where the shallow end of the pool is. Just as you would with small children, safeguard Bassets by limiting access to pools.

Basset Hounds and Children

Bassets make great pets for children. Adult Basset Hounds are large enough for the play of even enthusiastic children. Bassets are low on the list of dog breeds that often bite children. They are also low concerning domination and aggressiveness. Bassets aren't going to be as active as some terrier breeds, but neither will they be constantly jumping up on small children and knocking them down.

Note: While a great pet for children, care must be taken to keep children from jumping on the back of a Basset Hound or attempting to ride them. The skeletal structure of Basset Hounds is different from most other breeds and they must be protected from injuries that could be serious.

Children should always realize and remember that Basset Hounds were and are trailing hounds. They go where their noses lead them. If a Basset is allowed to range freely in a neighborhood or on a farm, it could follow an interesting scent away from its home. At the very least, the Basset could become lost. At worst, it could become injured or killed while single-mindedly following a scent. All doors and gates must *always* be closed and children need to know this will protect their pet.

Basset Hounds and Other Pets

Bassets are very good with other animals. They easily learn to share a household with cats and with other animals. Being bred to work cooperatively with other hounds in a pack, Bassets have an innate lack of aggressiveness.

Some kennels that raise Bassets have proven the good-natured side of the breed. It is not uncommon for several stud dogs to be kept together right in the same run and sharing the same dog house. This is also true of brood bitches. Puppies, even puppies of different ages, can often be housed together after they have been weaned and are awaiting new homes. There are few other breeds that could safely be housed in this manner.

Bassets in a household are the same as the breeding animals are. Their sweet nature and easy-going attitudes make them good house pets in homes where other animals reside.

Bassets as Guard Dogs

Bassets generally love everybody. They aren't much as guard dogs and don't even bark in a watchdog manner very often. Owners of Bassets

This Basset puppy and its feline friend can get along well together, especially if they are introduced while both are still young.

should depend on something other than their sorrowful-looking hounds to protect home and property.

Bassets are easy dogs to steal. They will even follow friendly strangers if allowed to do so. Bloodhounds and Bassets are first cousins. A Bloodhound story also fits for Basset Hounds: This Bloodhound was bred and trained to track fleeing prisoners or criminals. The hound's handler released the dog from its harness and the Bloodhound raced well ahead and caught up with the fugitive. The fugitive and the dog went on together. The Bloodhound was sold in the next town and this gave the prisoner enough money to make good his escape!

BASSET ASSET

Bassets do best as indoor pets. Long walks on a leash or good fenced-in yards help keep a Basset healthy and safe.

CARING FOR YOUR BASSET HOUND

The Basset is a scent hound that does best if he lives inside with his human owners. He is short of stature, but long on charm. The breed needs to be safe-guarded from wandering away from home and also needs consistent feeding. Medical issues, while not many, require regular veterinary visits.

Bassets don't want much. They want a place to sleep, food, water, and an occasional pat or a friendly word. A few more things are required to give Bassets adequate care. As trailing hounds they need to be confined in some manner all the time to keep them from following a trail away from home and family and possibly into harm's way. This confinement can be inside the house, in a fenced backyard or kennel run, on a leash when out on walks, or through proper training.

Like most breeds of dogs, the Basset has a special set of needs that a responsible owner should endeavor to meet.

Housing—Inside and Outside

The best way to keep Bassets, or any other dogs, in your home is to make use of a cage, crate, or carrier (see The Cage/Crate/Carrier, page 48). Dogs are naturally denning creatures. They will, if left to their own devices, find some place in your home to serve as their own, personal den. This place might be under a table in an out-of-the-way place, in a closet, or even behind a piece of furniture. Using a crate or carrier allows you to establish where the dog's den will be.

✔ Cages, crates, and carriers have revolutionized the way that house dogs can be made more comfortable and house-trained.

Not only does a dog instinctively need a place of its own, dogs also don't like to mess up these places by voiding waste there. Making use of these two instincts can help your Basset become a much better house pet. Even if he goes outside to a doghouse and fenced yard, a cage/crate/carrier is one of the best investments you can make.

✔ Although most Basset fans believe their favorite breed should be house-trained and live in the house with its owners, your Basset can function well both inside and outside the home. A fenced yard with a snug doghouse can be a good place for your Basset to stay on those very rare times when he is not with you.

If a fenced yard is not possible, a fenced kennel run with a doghouse may work. Without some fenced outside area, your Basset must either stay inside or go outside only when you are along. Because of their potential to roam away from home following a trail, no Basset can simply be put outside in complete safety.

The doghouse should be placed out of direct sunlight. There are many designs, but the best house will have a way for the dog to get out of direct drafts. In cold climates your Basset should probably be inside with you unless his house is thoroughly insulated and adequately ventilated. Warm areas require that the dog-house have more ventilation.

Exercising Your Basset

Bassets have only moderate exercise needs. Care should be taken with puppies and very young adults not to overdo exercise to avoid causing damage to still developing bones and muscles.

One of the best ways to exercise your Basset is to go for walks with the dog during relief

Bassets need regular, but moderate, outside exercise.

breaks. Both dog and owner can benefit from such regular strolling, with steps to match those of the Basset.

If your Basset spends much time in a fenced backyard, he will usually get enough exercise, but additional activities require added exercise to keep a Basset in shape. A Basset that hunts,

is a breeding animal, is a show dog, or is an obedience performer will need to be in good condition for these extra roles.

Moderate exercise is always needed as a way to battle that great canine killer, obesity. With a sensible diet, exercise can help Bassets keep off those extra pounds that can also cripple a long-bodied dog over time.

BASSET ASSET

Bassets are often very poor swimmers, if they can swim at all. Care must be taken to keep Bassets away from swimming pools, lakesides, or ponds where one slip might cost your dog's life.

Special Basset Hound Care

Your Basset is low to the ground; therefore, problems can sometimes result on the dog's undercarriage. Females may have scratches or abrasions on their teats. Males may have similar injuries on the sheath that protects their penis.

BASSET ASSET
Bassets usually have deep wrinkles or flews
that require extra attention and cleaning.

Regularly check the underside of your Basset to
be certain that no harm has befallen your low-
slung pet.

Bassets will need special feeding to avoid
age-related problems in youngsters or obesity
in older dogs (see Feeding Your Basset, page
71). Poor feeding practices can also do harm to
the skeletal development of your Basset. Make
nutrition for your dog a high priority item and
learn how to avoid problems that start in the
food bowl and could result in a shortened life
for your Basset Hound.

Note: Remember that as a scent hound, your
Basset can trail itself away from home. Protect
your pet from becoming another lost dog.

*Basset faces need regular cleaning with soft,
damp cloths. This is also a good time
to check your Basset's ears, jowls, and eyes.*

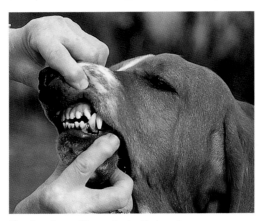

*Caring for a Basset's teeth involves owner
check-ups on a weekly basis and
professional attention each time your
dog visits the veterinarian.*

Traveling with Your Basset

Your Basset may not be the easiest pet with which to travel, but you can take trips with your dog. The safety and comfort of your Basset Hound should always be your first consideration. If the dog is very young or very old, or if some health problem exists, you may want to skip the trip or leave your hound at home.

One key rule is that your Basset should always travel in his crate or carrier—riding without restraint in a moving vehicle can be dangerous. Sharp curbs, sudden stops, or even minor traffic accidents can cause a dog to become a canine missile flying around in the car at surprisingly high speed and velocity. Do your Basset a favor and keep him in a carrier.

Traveling by Automobile

Car travel with a Basset Hound is not as difficult as air travel, but there are some good suggestions to follow:

1. Remember to use a carrier or a doggy safety harness whenever your Basset is riding in a car.

2. On longer trips stop every hour or so to give your Basset a breather, a drink of water, and a chance to relieve himself. Whenever you make these rest stops, always keep your Basset on a leash.

When traveling with a Basset, puppy or adult, it is very important to make certain that the pet is safeguarded from sudden stops and swerves. The best way to do this is with a cage/carrier just like your pet has as a sleeping place at home.

3. *Never leave your Basset in a parked car, even with windows rolled down, during the day when temperatures are as high as 60°F (16°C).*

4. Check with auto clubs and with national motel-hotel chains to discover places that allow pets to stay with their owners in their rooms. Don't try to sneak your Basset into a motel or hotel. In many places this is against the law.

Boarding Your Basset

If you can't take your Basset with you, you may be able to board your pet. Some boarding options are

1. Ask your veterinarian or pet supply store about reputable pet sitters that they can recommend. These pet sitters should be licensed, bonded, and able to provide references from pet owners they have worked for. Always check out these references carefully before entrusting your dog and your home to a stranger.

2. You and your Basset Hound may have a friend, neighbor, or family member who can care for your pet. Your Basset Hound could go for a visit or even stay at home and be cared for under this arrangement.

3. Your veterinarian can probably put your Basset up for a few days. This might also be a good time for a thorough checkup.

4. There are some excellent boarding kennels in most areas. These kennels are accredited with the American Boarding Kennel Association (ABKA) (see Information, page 93).

Trimming Toenails

Bassets, because of their high ratio of weight to height put a lot of stress on their feet. More active dogs, running over stones or on concrete surfaces, may wear down their toenails. Bassets will need their owners' help to avoid foot problems resulting from overgrown toenails.

Toenail trimming should begin when you first get a Basset puppy and should continue regularly at intervals of every ten days to two weeks for the entire life of the dog. Some dogs, especially those that have not had their nails trimmed from early puppyhood, may be skittish about having their feet fooled around with. By starting early, gradually, gently, and regularly, Bassets can learn that trimming is nothing to fear.

Basset owners should not fear nail trimming either. You can trim your pet's nails yourself with a good pair of trimmers. There are two kinds of nail trimmers, the scissors type and the guillotine type. The scissors nail trimmers are similar to snips used to trim metal or branches. The guillotine nail trimmers require placing the nail through an opening and snipping it off with the blade that goes downward.

Your veterinarian can show you how to trim your Basset's nails. Practice on round toothpicks until you cut off just the tip of the nail, avoiding the "quick" or center of the nail that contains a vein. This vein will bleed if you cut the nail too short.

When you check your dog's nails, always check the feet and toes for cuts, bruises, foreign materials such as splinters, and other potential problems. Your Basset will need to be given regular care for both grooming and health reasons.

Brushing Your Basset

Thoroughly brush your Basset Hound with a grooming mitt or a brush with bristles. Shedding coats will require either a shedding rake or a slicker brush to get out as much dead hair as possible. Starting with the head, carefully but gently brush the dog repeatedly. Use a fine-toothed metal comb for sensitive areas and places the brush or slicker cannot easily handle.

Giving Your Basset a Bath

As with their toenails, Basset Hounds should be bathed early in their lives to get them accustomed to this routine event. Breed experts point out that teaching a Basset to submit to its bath when it weighs 5 pounds (2.25 kg) is better than waiting until the dog weighs 50 pounds (23 kg). Baths should only be often enough to keep your Basset clean. Too many baths will dry a dog's skin and coat.

Along with regular use of a slicker brush and a regular bristle brush, a grooming mitt, sometimes called a "hound glove" can be used to groom the Basset's short, but thick, coat.

YOUR BASSET

Bathtime for a Basset should not be a long, drawn-out procedure. Using a very mild dog shampoo and warm water, wash the dog, paying special attention to thorough rinsing. Dry the dog carefully with thick towels or with an electric hair dryer, being careful not to burn the dog in the process.

Eyes: The Basset Hound's eyes are large and soap will irritate them. Keep soap and soapy water out of the eyes. Use a sterile petrolatum ophthalmic ointment as a precautionary step to protect your Basset's eyes. After the bath use a regular over-the-counter eyewash with a soft cloth or a cotton ball to gently wipe the eyes to make certain that no bath residue remains.

Ears: Use a similar process with the Basset Hound's ears. Be certain to keep shampoo and soapy water out of the ears. Some breeders and groomers put cotton balls in the ear canals to insure that no water gets in there. Because the Basset ears are so large and hang so low they get covered with dirt, bits of food, and other foreign material. Ears should get special cleaning attention both at bathtimes and in between. Using cotton with a mild astringent, or handy wipes used for human babies, thoroughly clean the ears, but only up to the cotton balls (which should be removed after each bath) that block the ear canals.

Basset ears deserve a daily check to see that they are free from parasites, like ear mites and ticks, and that they don't have small injuries or ear problems. Start checking and washing your Basset's ears while it is still a puppy and the process will be not only healthful for the dog, but less of a struggle for you.

The Basset Hound's long ears should be checked daily—it is helpful to have one person steady the dog's head while another person cleans or applies medication to the dog's ears.

Bassets and Tooth Care

Another part of grooming your Basset involves keeping the dog's teeth and gums in good health. Inexperienced dog owners would do well to have any excessive tartar on their pet's teeth removed by a veterinarian. With some experience, you can not only brush your Basset's teeth, but also do minor tartar removal with a tartar scraper.

Every time you check your Basset's eyes and ears, take a moment to check his teeth. Look for tartar, but also for foreign objects such as bits of food or wood slivers. Dog biscuits and various types of chew toys can help reduce tartar buildup but can't be expected to remove all tartar or replace regular dental care.

ADOPTING A BASSET HOUND

One of the most rewarding aspects of pet ownership stems from the opportunity to find a homeless dog and give it a whole new future. Through no fault of their own, a good number of Basset Hounds end up homeless. Finding a new home for such a Basset can be one of the best things any friend of dogs can ever do.

Many Bassets become homeless, often through no fault of their own. Dogs and puppies lose their owners through a wide variety of circumstances. Some Bassets trail themselves away from home and become lost. Neglect and human incompetence can play a part. Owner death, divorces, transfers to pet-unfriendly locations, and other situations leave numerous Basset Hounds of all ages in need of a new start, a new family, and a new future.

BASSET ASSET

Bassets are sometimes chosen simply because they are appealing and cute. Much more is required if you want to give a Basset Hound a good home.

Rescue Organizations

Most dog breeds and many breed types have volunteers who make it their concern to find homes for animals that, for one reason or another, require a new home. These groups fall under the general category of rescue organizations. Such organizations work closely with humane societies and other animal shelters to find people for new pets and for the pets in need of new people. These selfless volunteers help locate lost pets, foster those with no homes, and carefully place canines in new settings.

Basset Hounds have been blessed with a large number of rescue organizations. There is a direct correlation between a breed's popularity, its appeal, and its fad status and the number of dogs that may be surrendered for adoption or that become homeless. Bassets

Connecting loving adopters with Bassets in need of homes has become the focus for rescue groups.

have a loveable hangdog quality that endears them to many potential dog owners. Some of these potential owners may become competent and caring, but others fail at the role of Basset owner, which can result in an innocent pet in a bad situation.

Careful Concern

In order that Bassets in need of a new life with a new family get the best possible outcome, good rescue organizations take great care in checking out the people who may want to adopt their charges. Potential adopters should not be surprised when their backgrounds, living arrangements, and experience with other Bassets or other dogs are checked out. Rescue groups want to make as sure as possible that

the Basset they adopt out today doesn't become homeless again in the future when things don't work out in the new home. Just as responsible dog breeders want to make certain that their dogs and puppies go to the best possible homes, so do rescue organizations want to get the best for their home-needing Bassets.

Unlike most animal shelters, many rescue groups don't maintain kennels where people come to look at potential adoptees. Rescue

BASSET ASSET
Bassets are often left homeless when a careless owner learns that the dog isn't a stuffed animal to be taken off a shelf when it is convenient to do so.

CHECKLIST

Rescue Group Requirements

Before a family or individual can adopt a homeless Basset Hound, several requirements are stressed:

✔ All Bassets are spayed or neutered. No breedable males or females are adopted. (Young puppies are adopted on the proviso that they must be spayed or neutered as soon as is medically advisable.)

✔ Thorough medical exams are conducted and any health issues are recognized and dealt with where possible.

✔ Potential new homes are inspected for suitability. Most rescue organizations insist that any adopted Bassets will be inside dogs sharing the living space of their new owners.

✔ Prospective adopters should have Basset-safe environments (fenced yards are very positive), and such potential owners must understand the needs of dogs in general and the specific needs of Bassets.

✔ Rescue groups have charges for adoption that help to defray the care and feeding of their adoptees. These charges are reasonable and help to establish the value of the Basset Hound in the minds of a potential new home.

✔ A potential Basset adopter should have a veterinarian already lined up for the arrival of the new pet. Such medical attention for a Basset is wise and expected by the rescue organization.

✔ Many groups will expect follow-up reports and/or visits with the new pet owners and their adopted Basset Hounds. Such requirements are usually thoroughly spelled out in the adoption agreement signed by the rescue organization and the new adopter.

groups generally utilize a network of foster homes that not only give Bassets a place to live, but also help identify problems that should be addressed healthwise and in socialization and training. These foster homes, sometimes Basset adopters themselves, provide a stable base for a prospective pet from which it can be successfully placed in a new home.

Rescue Success

As with many other breeds, Basset Hound rescue organizations have had great degrees of success throughout their locales. Not every new home works out for every Basset and not every Basset works out for its new home. Rescue groups help minimize such problems with their careful assessments of the potential adopters. Some Bassets do well in a second new home experience.

The Adoption Option

For the average individual or family interested in a Basset as a pet, adoption is an excellent choice. There are many adoptable Bassets available and the rescue groups are an absolute

wellspring of information and help for anyone wanting a positive Basset experience.

Backyard (often careless and ignorant) breeders, puppy mills, and the "breed-for-greed" crowd have sometimes seized upon the adorable Basset as a money maker. Unfortunately, many of the Basset Hounds produced in such settings have health issues and other problems that prove extremely troublesome for inexperienced and often naïve buyers. Breeding of Bassets (or any other dogs) is best left to experienced breeders that have the good of the breed and the subsequent pet owners at heart.

Many people who become Basset Hound owners in an impulsive, "Oh-let's-get-one"

manner are among the first to neglect their new pets and ultimately be forced to surrender them to humane societies and animal shelters. Getting any new pet, and especially a complex dog like the Basset Hound, should never be a spur-of-the-moment decision. Yet for many dog owners, that is precisely what happens and rescue organizations are called upon to undo the damage and heartache caused.

Finding an Adoptable Basset

Fortunately, rescue organizations for Bassets (and for dogs that have some Basset in their genetic makeup—such as the Bagel—a Basset/

Beagle cross) are located throughout the United States and many other countries. Animal shelters may be able to help connect a prospective adopter with a rescue group (if the shelter has no suitable candidates for adoption). National Basset clubs through the American Kennel Club probably have organization names in locales around the United States. Simply going on the Internet can uncover a wealth of rescue sources and information.

It is important to remember that many excellent Basset pets (of all ages and both genders) are available to the right homes, using the animal shelters and Basset rescue groups. Countless Bassets have been successfully placed in new homes. One may be waiting just for you!

BASSET ASSET

Bassets without homes end up in animal shelters or in rescue groups that strive diligently to put the right dog and the right home together.

SELECTING A BASSET HOUND

As with many popular dog breeds, the Basset Hound does not fit in equally well with every home setting or dog-human situation. Before you decide to make your next companion animal a Basset, there are a number of considerations you should address—failing to do so can make you and an innocent pet miserable.

Before you consider bringing a Basset Hound into your life, give the matter a great deal of thought. Any pet will need your love and your attention. A Basset Hound will need your special attention to keep it safe and healthy.

Not Just Another Pretty Face

Humans have produced over 300 separate breeds of dogs worldwide. Some of these breeds are quite utilitarian in purpose; the Greyhound and the Basset are good examples of such breeds. Both breeds also have gained many

Choosing a Basset Hound, puppy or adult, on impulse is a bad decision to make. Sure they are appealing, but do you really know what owning a Basset involves?

friends for their pet qualities, but their utilitarian aspects remain, and must be considered.

The Basset is a charmingly sad-looking breed that wins people over by its appearance and sweet disposition. The Basset isn't overly active, too demanding, or prone to moodiness. The Basset is a hound. As a hound its primary instincts are to follow scents. Following scents takes precedence over most other aspects of Basset life, other than sleeping and eating.

The Basset and its bigger cousin, the Bloodhound, have the best scenting abilities of all dogs. Both breeds descended from centuries-old hunting hound breeds. Both breeds are wrinkled and have long ears, characteristics that contribute to trailing by wafting the scent toward the hound's nose and, in the case of the wrinkling, retaining the scent to help keep the hound aware of it.

The appearance of the Basset may be appealing. Bassets may be among the most photogenic, and photographed, dogs. They may be used as logos and pitch-dogs for various products, but Bassets are still hounds. Failing to consider that a pet Basset, generations removed from hunting, is other than a hound is an error. An error that can potentially bring harm to the gentle, homely handsome Basset.

Being a Good and Consistent Dog Owner

All breeds of dogs need and deserve owners that will be consistent. Bassets may need this consistency even more than some other breeds.

One of the greatest mistakes a dog owner can make is failing to be consistent. Bassets (and all other dogs) deserve an owner who does the right thing, the right way, each and every time.

Because of the possibility of health problems brought on by poor feeding practices, the constant threat of a Basset following an interesting smell away from home, the patience needed in some Basset training, and the highly specialized physique of the Basset, consistency in these areas is essential.

Bassets will eat many things but they will thrive only on a carefully balanced diet. Bassets can be happy inside or outside the home, but they must have a secure environment that keeps them at home. Bassets weren't bred from centuries of successful house pets. Training for a Basset is a little more involved and requires a little more attention than it does with some breeds. The long spine and almost gnarled front legs of the breed demand special arrangements to keep them from being injured in doing even everyday things that other breeds do.

To be a good and consistent Basset owner, you will need to do the same things, the same way, each time. In feeding, kenneling, training, and safeguarding, the Basset will do best if its owner is aware of these special needs and then consistent in filling them.

Searching for the Right Dog

Finding the right Basset Hound requires some Basset behavior on your part! You must become a determined hunter of just the right Basset. You must get the correct mental picture of just what you are seeking and stay on the trail until you have found what you want.

Whether you purchase a Basset puppy or adopt an older dog, try to see as many Bassets as possible. In this way, you will have a varied mental picture of lots of dogs from which to pick.

✔ There are many potential places to obtain a Basset Hound. There are newspaper classified ads in most cities that often have Bassets listed. There are magazines such as *Dog Fancy* and *Dog World* that have advertisements by Basset kennels and breeders. The Basset Hound Club of America (see Information, page 93) can help you find Basset breeders in your area.

✔ Visit as many dog shows as you can. You can see Bassets, and many other breeds, as they compete. You will almost certainly be able to meet some Basset fans at dog shows who will help you understand Bassets and possibly help you in your search.

✔ Most dog experts believe that in most circumstances you will have a better chance of finding the right dog if you go to breeders that have a reputation for quality. Buying a Basset

from the local newspaper classifieds is not unlike buying a used car from the same source. You may find just the right pet, but you may not. Breeders specialize in pure bred dogs. They know that selling poor-quality, unhealthy, or defective dogs or puppies will injure their credibility.

A Male or Female?

Basset Hounds of either sex usually make excellent pets. Males are a little harder to house-train, but have a few more skills as early-warning watchdogs. Female Bassets are a little smaller than males. They tend to be easier to train and house-train. Unspayed females (see Spaying and Neutering, page 43) will go into season or heat approximately twice a year with the potential of a litter of unwanted puppies as a result.

As you search for a Basset Hound with whom to share your life, remember that there are adoptable dogs of all ages that would love to belong to and with you.

Whether you choose a male Basset or a female is largely going to be your call. Both sexes have sweet dispositions. Both are good with children, but both are still trailing hounds that could wander away from home if not supervised or sufficiently fenced.

An Older Basset or a Puppy?

Adult Bassets are very adaptable (and adoptable) under most situations. One breeder said, "Many Bassets feel right at home with whoever is feeding them." Problems arise with adult dogs when they have been mistreated, when they have not been trained, or when new owners have unreasonable expectations about Bassets in general, and this Basset in particular.

An un-housetrained kennel hound or a dog that was always outside in its previous existence may not adapt well to life in a small apartment. An overfed and obese urban house pet may not last long if suddenly thrust into the home of an avid rabbit hunter who wants the dog to vigorously hunt throughout rabbit season.

Common sense is especially important in choosing an adult dog of any breed. While Bassets don't tend to have all the difficulties that some breeds do in living with new owners, they do need new homes that understand the adjustment process.

Basset puppies are adorable. One problem facing the Basset breed, as a whole, is the cuteness of Basset puppies that contributes to impulse buyers who don't really understand Bassets or Basset owning.

Puppies require a great deal of time to help them learn what is expected of them. Basset puppies require special care in feeding so that they do not develop certain forms of lameness that afflict the breed. They also need to be kept from jumping, stair climbing, and too much exercise, all of which can cause young Basset Hounds physical problems.

Puppies are also moldable to what a family or an individual wants in a pet. They may require more attention at the beginning of their lives, but Basset puppies can grow up with their families, which is a great part of owning a pet. Basset puppies grow quickly, but they are also slow to mature.

Some adult Bassets may be available from breeders. Some Bassets are rescued from bad environments and may be available for adoption into a knowledgeable and responsible home. One can bypass many trying days of puppy ownership with an adult Basset, but greater care must be taken to understand why an adult is available. Bad habits in an adult are much harder to break than is the instilling of correct habits in a puppy.

Pet, Show, Field Dog, or All Three?

That the Basset usually makes an excellent pet to the right owner is well known. The Basset also has a good record in the show ring.

Their original hunting role is still very much in evidence in many Basset Hounds. There are AKC champion Bassets that have done well in field trials and as rabbit dogs. Such versatility is not common in any breed, but the potential in many Bassets is there.

Pet-quality puppies are those that have some cosmetic flaw that will not allow them to pursue a show dog career. These puppies, when healthy and genetically sound, are still prime candidates for a home seeking a pet Basset. The price for such a puppy will be less than for puppies with show dog potential, but always beware of "bargain basement" Bassets.

Show puppies are usually not readily for sale. Most litters bred by qualified breeders in most breeds may have only one really good show prospect, if they have any at all. Never expect to buy the top puppy. Good prospects are rare enough to make them valuable in more ways than financially. Breeders will want to keep these puppies for themselves or have them in the hands of people who will show the youngster to the limit of its potential as an exhibition-quality show dog.

Carefully consider just what you want your Basset to be, *before* you go out to buy one. If you aren't interested in showing or hunting with your Basset, find the best pet-quality Basset available that will serve as a pet and as a member of your family for the next decade and more.

Knowing if the Basset Hound Is Right for You

✔ Bassets are hounds. Expecting the alertness of one of the terrier breeds, the protectiveness of one of the guard dog breeds, the demand for affection and attention of one of the toy breeds, or the ease of training and versatility of one of the breeds that top the obedience trial title winners' list, will only make you unhappy with a Basset. To expect the Basset to be more than a Basset is patently unfair to the breed and to an individual dog.

✔ Bassets are more than just an appealing dog to capture the oohs and ahhs of passersby on the street. Bassets need special care to have happy, healthy lives.

✔ Bassets are much larger in length and breadth of body than most people realize. Their lack of height has made some people think of the Basset as a small dog, which it most definitely is not!

✔ Bassets have such acute senses of smell that careful, extra thorough cleaning of urine or feces voided inside is essential. Dogs are instinctively driven to reuse elimination spots. If a keen scenting Basset can find enough traces of former mistakes made on a carpet, it may decide that if this spot was good once, perhaps it will serve this purpose again.

✔ Bassets must be kept at home by sturdy fences and gates that correctly close and latch each time. Singleminded tracking can lead a Basset to become lost or even to be killed by an automobile while following an interesting scent.

✔ Basset puppies require extra help in growing up strong and fit. Though heavy in bone mass, young Bassets shouldn't receive vitamin supplements unless prescribed by a veterinarian with experience in treating Basset Hounds.

✔ No dog should be simply tied or chained to a tree and left alone except at feeding time. While Bassets do well in kennel arrangements with proper exercise, they won't do well chained or tied all their lives.

✔ Bassets are prone to obesity that can be torturous to their long spines. Feeding care is probably more important, with old or young Bassets, than it is with most other dog breeds.

If you can fit such a breed into your life style, providing for its needs and restraints, then the Basset may be the right dog for you.

Knowing If You Are Right for the Basset Hound

✔ Do you want a Basset Hound as a fashion accessory or do you want a real dog with many good qualities as a pet?

✔ Have you owned other dogs that can serve as a reference point on how to treat a Basset?

✔ Are you so enamored with another type of dog that the laid-back nature of the Basset will become a dissatisfaction?

✔ Are you willing to invest the time and money to search for and find the right Basset for you and your family?

✔ Do you and your family have enough time and enough space to create the right environment for a Basset?

✔ Are you willing to impress upon your family and guests that the Basset requires that doors and gates be securely shut, no table scraps should be given, and care should be taken in picking up this long-bodied breed?

✔ Will you, or another responsible adult, be able to stay at home the first few days after you obtain a Basset puppy to help the newcomer settle in?

✔ Will you commit to regular veterinary visits for your Basset? Are you willing to follow instructions about health care your Basset may need throughout its life?

If you can honestly answer these questions (and others that may be posed to you by Basset

Bassets have an elegance and beauty all their own and their worth as canine companions is one of their top attributes.

breeders), you may be a suitable owner for the right Basset.

Choosing a Basset Puppy

After determining no rescue Basset will do, you have carefully searched and found a reputable breeder who can give you a look at a litter of Basset puppies. You and your family have discussed the sex of the puppy you want, and whether you want a puppy with show potential or just a pet puppy. You may have decided that you will want to field trial or hunt with your Basset when it is older and you have chosen a breeder who has produced Bassets that have done well in these activities. You may have decided that you want a specific color. You have all the prerequisites charted out so that

you can find a puppy that comes close to what you are seeking.

The only problem with this scenario is that it fails to consider the charm of young Bassets. One couple was convinced that they wanted a red and white female puppy with some show potential and came home with a tricolor (black with white and brown) pet-quality, male puppy. This couple has been very happy with this fine pet. They do vow that their next Basset will be a red and white female with show potential— probably.

If you don't want to consider other sexes, qualities, or colors, ask the breeder to show you only the ones that fit your specifications. You must decide that your specifications are more of a priority than seeing a puppy that really pulls at your heartstrings.

Preparation is essential before you bring your Basset Hound puppy home. Preplanning will make life much simpler for both of you!

It is wise to look at several litters, if possible. Try hard not to choose a puppy from the first litter that you see. You may come back and buy this puppy, but give yourself the option of comparing as many puppies (and their mothers, and their surroundings) as possible.

What You Should Expect

You should expect to pay several hundred dollars for a good-quality Basset puppy; show-potential puppies could be as high as $1,000 or more. Different prices are the norm in different parts of the country, but you should

Basset Hound puppies need to sleep in their cages or crates. Whining and whimpering during the first nights in a new home will pass.

always seek quality, and expect to pay a fair price for it.

Most reputable breeders will be as concerned about you as a potential owner of one of their puppies as you should be about them as the source of a puppy that will become a member of your family for years into the future. If you have become friends with some Basset breeders from dog shows during your search for the right Basset, you might ask these breeders if they would say that yours seems to be a good potential home for a Basset.

You also may want to see some references or records concerning the breeder from whom you are considering purchasing a puppy. Through this Basset you and this breeder will be linked together for years to come. Both of you should

be content with the arrangement. Before choosing a Basset puppy from any source you should have access to:

1. Health Records: These records will reflect all the information from any veterinary visits, what treatments have been given (and for what), and a dated listing of what vaccinations the puppy has had.

2. The form that acknowledges that this puppy comes from a litter that has been duly registered as pure bred with the American Kennel Club.

3. The puppy's pedigree or family tree that shows its ancestry. The right breeder will have this pedigree and will be proud to point out the outstanding progenitors of your potential puppy.

Young Bassets need consistent care. Carefully evaluate your home environment to make things easier for a new and often uneasy puppy.

potential Basset owner. To guarantee this fitness, there are some documents that a breeder may require of you!

1. A spay/neuter agreement for pet-quality puppies. Only the very best Basset Hounds should ever be allowed to be bred. If you have specifically designated that you want a pet puppy, a wise breeder will want to make certain that this puppy doesn't reproduce. This is a perfectly reasonable expectation. You will have to get a female spayed or a male neutered and show proof, signed by the attending veterinarian.

2. A return agreement that specifies that should your plans change and you can't keep your Basset, that the dog will be returned to the owner instead of being disposed of in another manner, such as, sold, given away, taken to an animal shelter, or euthanized. This agreement is at the option of the breeder, but the desire to maintain positive control over a Basset that was sold to you tells you a lot about the quality of the breeder you have chosen.

4. Test results for the parents of this puppy concerning certain inheritable conditions. Chief among these is the result of screening for Canine Hip Dysplasia (CHD). These tests and others are conducted on adult dogs and while they are not conclusive guarantees that this puppy will be free from these ailments, parental test results are somewhat predictive in detecting the total genetic health of the mother and father of a specific puppy. The presence of such test results also is an indicator that this breeder has complied with accepted safeguards to assure that the puppies you are seeing are as genetically healthy as it is reasonably possible to determine.

5. Other documents that a Basset breeder may want to add, such as care and feeding hints, Basset clubs' names and addresses, and other items this breeder deems important.

What Should Be Expected of You

Many reputable breeders won't let you buy a puppy unless they are sure of your fitness as a

Christmas Puppies

Everyone has seen or imagined a happy child on Christmas morning as it is surprised by a new puppy. This is, in reality, a most unhappy scene, at least for the puppy involved. Basset puppies need a lot of early care, socialization, and settling in to give them the best possible start in their new families. Christmas is a time of hustle and bustle in most households and a bewildered puppy can get lost in all the activity.

Unless the Basset puppy is the only gift given, wait until after Christmas to bring a new family member into your home. That doesn't mean that you can't buy books, or videos about Bassets to give as a gift foretelling the arrival of the puppy later.

Be wise rather than sentimental regarding Christmas puppies and surprise puppies given any time of the year. Basset puppies deserve to be cared for and prepared for to have the happiest possible outcome.

Spaying and Neutering

There are millions of unwanted dogs and puppies available today. Spaying your female Basset or neutering your male Basset is a sure way of not contributing to this glut of sadly surplus canines. Even if the breeder doesn't require it, unless you have a champion-quality show or hunting Basset, have the dog rendered unable to reproduce.

Many people feel they are depriving a pet of something wonderful when they spay or neuter, but that is all wrong! Bassets are not easy to breed. There are many kinds of problems that can happen to unspayed females, among them twice-a-year heat seasons, tumors, false pregnancies, and unwanted litters. Males will become better pets in that they won't react to the scents of in-season bitches in your neighborhood.

Spaying and neutering is a definitely positive thing for you to do for your pet, yourself, and for the world of dogs in general! (It is true that American Kennel Club rules prohibit spayed or neutered dogs from some performance events.)

YOUR NEW BASSET HOUND PUPPY

A new puppy will definitely be a work-in-progress and so will you as a new Basset Hound owner. Take great care to help this puppy (and you and your family) to get off to the best possible start. Do nothing impulsively as a new Basset owner. Every step will require your careful and knowledgeable attention. Study before you obtain a new Basset.

Before You Bring Your Basset Hound Home

The safety and comfort of your new Basset Hound should be your first considerations. You have already begun this process when you honestly viewed the suitability of a Basset as the right dog for you and your suitability as a Basset owner. By taking a serious approach to preparing for the new Basset in your life, you will greatly increase your chances of success as a Basset owner and the dog's chances of being happy and safe with you.

Special Considerations for Basset Safety

Along with swimming problems that many Bassets seem to have, the fact that the Basset is built so low to the ground, has long trailing ears, and deep creases or wrinkles can also bring special safety considerations.

If you hunt with your Basset or just take walks in the park, you should always be alert for broken glass, stinging or irritating insects, and other surface-level and injurious items that could cut a Basset's ears or scrape its underside. Also check the mouth, tongue, jowls, and chin, areas that may be down almost on the ground when a Basset is following a scent or just snuffling along.

Because of the deep wrinkles common in most Bassets, not only should the dog be gone over daily for allergies, rashes, and parasites, but the dog's facial skin should be checked for thorns, splinters, even sun exposure (especially in areas where the dog has white pigmentation on its face).

Bassets need lots of love and companionship. Sometimes, more than one puppy is a good idea.

Bringing Your Basset Home

After you have safety checked your home and eliminated as many potential dangers as possible, you are able to bring your Basset home. There are several important aspects to this first trip:

✔ Under most circumstances your Basset needs to ride in the safety of a carrier whenever it is in an automobile. For the first trip home a modification can be made in this rule. If your Basset is a young puppy, you can let a responsible member of your household carefully and gently cradle the young Basset in his or her arms. Be sure to include some old towels in case of motion sickness. Follow the recommendations for traveling with your pet in an automobile (see page 23). This personal touch will help the bewildered puppy feel more comfortable as it starts its life with you.

✔ When you arrive home with your new Basset, put the puppy on a leash and go immediately to the pre-selected relief spot. Wait there patiently until your puppy uses this area to urinate or defecate. Praise the youngster enthusiastically to make this natural activity a pleasant and memorable event. (To aid in getting the idea across as to what goes on at this specific site, you could bring some urine-soaked bedding or feces from its first home to "salt" the location.)

✔ After the puppy has conducted its business, you can then take it inside to begin making it feel at home with you. Don't let the youngster play too much. It has had a tiring trip.

✔ At the first sign of the puppy getting tired, take it and put it in its carrier (see The Cage/Crate/Carrier, page 48). A blanket that has some scent from home will help the Basset puppy identify with the carrier. You want to make certain that your puppy identifies the crate with being tired and wanting to sleep.

✔ Follow the same feeding schedule that the breeder used with the puppy, using the same food if at all possible.

The Adjustment Phase

A responsible adult will need to stay at home with the young Basset for the first few days to see that the puppy settles in and begins the adjustment to being in its new home with its new family.

The most difficult part of this adjustment time is usually the first few nights. Getting through these nights is crucial to the future success of this Basset in your household. Many puppies will naturally miss their mother and littermates. They are in a strange place and this is frightening to them. When puppies are frightened they generally whimper and cry because this brought attention and comfort.

You and your family are now your Basset puppy's family. When you place the puppy in its crate for the night you and every

BASSET ASSET

Bassets Hounds, adults or puppies, will need some time to adapt to a new home. Responsible pet owners understand this and do everything possible to help with the process.

person in your home must steel yourselves to the whimpers of the lonely puppy. What you do these first few nights can rarely be erased or undone. Your Basset must learn to sleep in its crate without having to be comforted by some human from its new family. If you fail to teach your Basset this key lesson, you may make the animal dependent on you every night for the rest of its life!

Your young Basset will become comfortable in its crate after it comes to understand that this is its special place within your home (see The Cage/Crate/Carrier, page 48). The first few nights the puppy will not be comfortable, but no member of your household can give in to feeling sorry for the puppy, going

Basset ownership, for the prepared and knowledgeable family, can be a load of fun and lots of good times.

and getting it, and holding it to stop its sorrow. Everyone must understand that a sad Basset puppy that endures a few days of loneliness before it adapts is much to be preferred to a sad adult Basset that cries every night. Dog pounds and animal shelters are full of dogs that never learned to sleep peacefully by themselves. Don't let your Basset become just like them!

There are some things that you can put in the crate with your Basset puppy that may help ease this temporary suffering. An old-fashioned hot water bottle, wrapped in a thick towel will provide a semblance of its mother's warmth. A nonelectric, ticking, old alarm clock can seem like her heartbeat. A radio placed near the crate or carrier, tuned to a talk station and on low volume can also be comforting to a puppy.

Place the puppy's crate not far from where you sleep but far enough that you aren't tempted to constantly talk to the puppy and where the whining and crying won't keep you awake. Let the baby Basset endure a few nights and it will learn that the crate is for sleep and it will rarely whine and cry again.

Be Consistent Right from the Start

Everything you do with the puppy should be consistent if it is to correctly learn what it has to do to please you. Owner inconsistency has ruined a multitude of dogs. If a behavior is wrong one time, it should be wrong the next time. If one activity is permitted and then it isn't, dogs become confused and sometimes resentful. Set rules and standards of behavior and let these be the same each time. Your puppy will learn much quicker this way.

The Cage/Crate/Carrier

Your Basset Hound will be a much better pet if you begin to crate-train the youngster from the moment it comes to live with you.

Crate-training takes advantage of one of the greatest truths about canines, that they are denning creatures. Left on their own, all dogs will seek to find some secluded area that can be rightfully their own place to sleep, relax, or just be out of the way. The crate is just such a denning place for your Basset.

Everyone in your home *must* understand that the carrier or crate is not a cruel thing used to imprison your Basset. Explain to each person that the carrier or crate is as natural for your pet as having a room of one's own is natural for human beings. Not only is crate-training not cruel, it helps the Basset puppy adjust to its new home, keeps it safe when the family must be away for a short while, and makes house-training much, much easier.

Part of the denning instinct that virtually all canines have is a second instinct that is equally strong and equally natural. In the wild canines are always careful to void their wastes away from where they have their den. Not only does this make the den a more pleasant place, it also keeps the smell of accumulated feces and urine from serving as a signal to other predators just where the den is. In your home your Basset will want to avoid eliminating wastes in the place where it sleeps—its crate. This instinct makes crate-training part of house-training.

House-training

Even if your Basset will stay outside sometimes, house-training your pet is a good idea. While it is true that Bassets are not among the top breeds in ease of house-training, they can become house-trained with the help of a persistent and consistent owner. Some hints for making house-training your Basset easier are:

BASSET ASSET

Bassets, while not the quickest on average to house-train, can and do eventually learn what they are supposed to do and where they are supposed to do it.

---

1. Start immediately when you get home with the puppy to introduce it to the right place for it to urinate and defecate. Use the same location *each* time you take your puppy out to void wastes. If your puppy's relief area is a public area, always be responsible and clean up solid wastes and dispose of them appropriately. If the relief spot is in your yard, occasional tidying up will keep the area inoffensive to humans but will maintain the needed scent for your Basset.

2. Crate-train your Basset puppy and take advantage of the natural habit that most dogs have in wanting to keep their den area clean.

3. Buy a crate that is large enough for the *adult* Basset and then partition it off so that it fits the size of the growing puppy. Too much room in a crate may cause a puppy to subdivide and make one corner of the crate into a bathroom. Just enough room for the dog to turn around and to sleep comfortably is all the space required.

4. *Always* praise your Basset with lots of pats and hugs *each* time it does what you want it to do at the relief site. *Never* punish or scold the puppy or dog at this important location. To do so will only confuse the pet and could undo some of the house-training lessons learned.

5. Time your puppy's meals with a trip outside. Young dogs have limited colon and bladder volume and taking food or water in generally means that some wastes will soon need to be going out.

6. Take your puppy outside as late as possible at night and as early as possible the next morning. Don't be unintentionally cruel and leave a puppy with a full bladder in its crate longer than you absolutely have to.

7. No matter how much you may want to house-train your Basset puppy, bladder control comes only with age. A young Basset under one year old, and some over a year old, may not be able to keep from making messes now and then. Know that this is going to happen and be prepared to effectively clean up the messes and find some odor-covering agent to neutralize the latent smell to stop future repetitions at this same spot.

8. When your puppy is out of its crate, watch it carefully. If it starts to look uncomfortable, comes to you in a plaintive manner, stays near the door, or starts circling or squatting, get it outside. Quickly and gently, and even if it has already begun to urinate or defecate, take the puppy out to the relief spot and

---

BASSET ASSET
Basset puppies need to be kept away from things that can hurt them. Electric wires, stairs, and small gnawable items are just such things.

---

wait until it goes there, reward it with praise, and come back in.

9. *Never* punish a puppy for making a mess. You can attempt to stop the act by firmly saying "*No*" or by clapping your hands in a way to break its concentration as you go out to the relief spot. Rubbing a puppy's nose in its waste is stupid, pointless, and counterproductive. Your puppy won't even know why you are doing this. *Never* strike a puppy with anything, not even the proverbial rolled-up newspaper.

10. Be consistent with your young Basset. Don't change relief spots. Don't wait to clean up a mistake. Don't yell at the puppy.

Always reward the puppy for doing what it should at the relief site.

Paper Training

A less effective and less efficient way to house-train is called *paper training*. Because Bassets, especially males, have more trouble becoming quickly house-trained, paper training may not be a very good alternative. But it is the only option that can be used for Basset owners, such as those on upper floors in apartment buildings, who can't rush their puppy out to a relief site quickly.

Bassets sometimes take a little longer to house-train. Be patient, especially with young males, and when and where to go will be learned to everyone's satisfaction.

Certainly give your Basset puppy time to settle in, but start training early. The lessons the youngster learns now should be the right ones.

Paper training involves placing layers of newspapers all over the floor of some easily cleaned room such as a laundry room or spare bathroom. Rather than having an outside elimination spot, the puppy has a relief room or a spot in a relief room.

Paper training does work when a Basset's owner must be away for several hours during the day, but paper training should always be only a substitute for the more effective outside method. Paper training breaks the rule against inconsistency in that sometimes inside is okay to void wastes, but other times outside is where it should be done.

Layers of paper are used so that the top layers may be picked up; leaving a clean surface that still has a scent for the young Basset to follow. Paper training doesn't work particularly well with the much preferred crate-training

approach. Taking a puppy out of its crate to another place inside the home can confuse the dog. Still, paper training can work, to a degree, with some Bassets.

The best way to view paper training is as a short-term, partial solution. By establishing a relief spot in the room and gradually making that spot smaller and smaller until it can be moved outside, paper training can serve part of the house-training function.

House-training your Basset may take a little longer, a little more patience, and a lot of consistency. It can be done. Most Basset experts firmly believe that all Basset puppies can be eventually house-trained if the owner follows this patience and consistency model. Combined with crate-training, Basset house-training efforts aren't really much more difficult than most breeds in the hound group.

Your new Basset will need a safe environment in which to grow up and flourish. How you make your puppy's living space safe depends largely on you and members of your household. Because of the low-profile stature of your Basset, special care must be taken at Basset-level to remove any items or conditions that can hurt or kill your new family member.

It is important to remember that *every* area, inside and outside, to which your Basset has access, must be thoroughly checked for possible dangers.

✔ Work from bottom upward. Get down on the floor and try to see dangers from the Basset's level. Look for things that could injure the puppy or that the puppy could swallow. Because owning a Basset should be a family affair, enlist your children in the task of being down on the floor looking for unsafe things.

✔ Look for sharp points at puppy-eye level, electrical outlets and extension chords that could cause instant death to a chewing puppy.

✔ Stabilize or remove any heavy things that could fall and crush a young puppy.

✔ Look for chemically treated areas where a young Basset could come in contact with noxious fumes or substances. Cleaning fluid residues, lead-based paints on old woodwork or furniture, forgotten ant or rat poison could easily be ingested by an unknowing youngster.

✔ It is especially important that Basset puppies *not* have access to steps, either going up or down. Trying to climb stairs and steps can do great damage to the developing skeletal systems of young Basset Hounds.

✔ Block off any balconies, porches, or risen hearths from which a puppy could fall.

✔ Close off any tight places behind televisions, heavy furniture, refrigerators, pianos, and so forth that could trap a young Basset who is only intent on following his nose.

✔ Eliminate access to any potential nooses that could catch a Basset puppy's head and cause strangulation in a frightened, struggling young dog. Some of these can be supports holding up railings,

There are dozens of everyday household items that can prove fatal to dogs and puppies. Seek out all of these items (and more) to create a nontoxic environment for your Basset Hound.

openings in trellises and fences, and other head-inviting gaps.

✔ Keep a Basset away from household cleaners, detergents, chemicals, and other killers that are often kept in cabinets and on low shelves, right at Basset level.

✔ If your dog or puppy can get to your garage or other places where your automobile is parked, be sure to thoroughly clean up spillages of gasoline and other fluids. *Especially* dangerous is antifreeze that has a smell and taste that dogs seem to love, and that is a deadly poison to them.

✔ Outside there are many potential dangers down low where Bassets live. Sharp wires, branches, edges, vents, wiring, and so on can be overlooked until your Basset is injured by running into one of them.

✔ There are many poisonous plants around many households. Some of these are azaleas, holly and its berries, milkweed, poison ivy, mistletoe, philodendron, jimson weed, and other regional wild, house, and garden plants.

✔ A preventive approach to Basset-proofing is to crate-train your pet (see The Cage/Crate/ Carrier, page 48) and then use the crate or an outside kennel area for those times when your Basset can't be adequately supervised or watched over.

✔ Swimming pools (see page 21), decorative fish ponds, even large containers that can collect water may be just enough to trap and drown a young puppy.

Most safety proofing is common sense, but by taking a carefully designed approach you will be less likely to overlook some danger. Prevention is always much easier than treatment or having to bury a puppy killed by a lack of forethought.

Pins, needles, thumbtacks, even coins, can cause harm to a puppy. An integral part of puppy-proofing centers on finding and removing such dangers from your home.

✔ For ease in house-training your young Basset, select a place where relief breaks to void wastes can be conveniently and quickly handled. Always using this location will help remind the young Basset what it is supposed to do at this spot.

Fenced yards, crates or carriers, and barriers to dangerous places within the home (stairs, landings, balconies, etc.) are all key elements in puppy-proofing where you and your Basset puppy will live.

TRAINING YOUR BASSET HOUND

While the Basset Hound is not in the rarified training air of the Border Collie and the Golden Retriever, this breed can definitely learn many commands. By stressing patience and consistency you should be able to create a very satisfactory canine companion out of your Basset Hound.

All Dogs Deserve Training

That the Basset is usually a calm and laid-back dog is true. That the Basset cannot benefit from becoming trained is *not* true. All dogs need and deserve to be trained. There will surely be times in every Basset's life when all that stands between the dog and danger is its training. Leashes break. Gates get left open. Bassets are still dogs and don't recognize all the possible dangers there are. Good training gives a dog owner one more way to control his or her Basset. Being able to control a powerful, though short, dog may someday save that dog's life.

Bassets are not the easiest dog for a beginner to train. Dog training classes and the help of experienced Basset breeders will always make this task less difficult. Bassets are

Every pet should have the benefit of good training. Don't deprive your Basset of the lessons he needs to be his best.

hounds. Hounds are bred to chase things, either in a pack or independently. Hounds generally learn by doing. Young hounds are usually paired with older dogs that know what they are chasing and how to do it. Other than coming back to their owners, many hounds now and down through the centuries never got a lot of extra training; none was usually required.

The top obedience dogs almost always have come from breeds that have do jobs that require quite a bit of training and have required such training for many generations. Retrievers and shepherds fill many of the top obedience spots because their jobs and their ancestors' jobs required them to understand fairly complex commands and behaviors. In a recent survey, which may or may not be correct, the Border Collie was ranked as the smartest of all canines and on the other end was the Afghan hound, which was originally bred to chase something.

Hounds, and Bassets in particular, aren't dumb dogs. Their lineage and activities require them to be smart in different ways from some other breeds. The Bloodhound, the breed that many experts link closely with the Basset in genetic heritage, is a rather good obedience dog. Bloodhounds have been trained in the very demanding task of finding fugitives and lost persons. Some Basset breeders believe the Basset could be developed to do the same job.

The Three Keys to Basset Training

The keys to training Bassets are consistency, persistency, and patience. The average novice Basset owner working with the average Basset

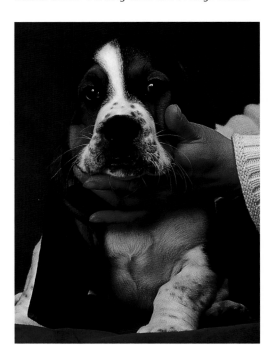

can use these three keys to achieve training success.

A dog trainer who does a lesson differently each time has no consistency. Such a trainer will fail because dogs, especially Bassets, will need to clearly understand what is required of them. Without such clarity dogs become confused and possibly resentful.

A dog trainer that gives up because training a Basset isn't as easy as it looks in a book or on a video lacks persistency. Training is a process, not a milestone. Bassets will need little refresher courses throughout their lives. A trainer lacking persistence will never go quite far enough to get a lesson across to his or her Basset.

A dog trainer without patience will never teach a Basset anything, except possibly to fear or hate the trainer. An impatient trainer often lashes out at the student for the teacher's inability to teach. Bassets are loving pets and will usually want to please their owners. Bassets do not learn to be obstinate. While they can be stubborn, that is where patience on the part of the trainer comes in. Without patience a Basset owner is doomed to own an untrained and probably frustrated Basset Hound.

General Training Tips

In addition to the more specific keys to training Bassets, there are several tips that can help with any dog. Some are the same for the Basset, but are important enough to bear repeating:

Your Basset's first and best teacher was its mother. Follow the training techniques of this exceptional trainer and you and your Basset Hound will have a good outcome.

Use the tenets of pack behavior to your training advantage. Remember that you and your family members are also members of the pack.

1. Praise enthusiastically: Your training role is to help your puppy achieve success and then to praise enthusiastically as a reward for that success. The best reward you can give your dog is praise. Some people use food as a reward. This may work for them, but what do you do when you don't have any food and you want to reward your puppy? Bassets don't need the extra food anyway.

2. Correct fairly and immediately: You want to get the desired response, not punish the puppy. A simple "*No*" or slight pressure on the lead and collar is enough. Immediate response is crucial for a puppy that has a short attention span; later correction won't be associated with the misdeed.

3. Practice consistent repetition: Your Basset will need to have a clear understanding of just what you want. Give the command the same way each time and expect the same result.

4. NEVER lose your temper: One angry outburst from you, directed at a bewildered puppy, could literally ruin this dog for any further training by making it fear you.

5. Be patient: Already highlighted as a key for training Bassets, patience is an important virtue in all aspects of dog ownership, but it is of greatest importance in training. The puppy isn't having trouble learning the commands to spite you; it simply may not understand what you want.

Pack Behavior

Basset Hounds, and all other canines, are pack animals. Bassets were bred for their pack attributes for hundreds of years. Trailing game in a pack with other Bassets is as natural as breathing for most Bassets. Pack behavior runs very strong in most scent hounds and is possibly strongest in Bassets. Even wild dogs and

wolves have a pack format to their lives. The pack forms the social hierarchy that controls most aspects of these canines' lives.

Pack behavior, once understood by a Basset owner, can be a great help in training a Basset. The first concept in understanding pack behavior is that of the "alpha male." Usually the strongest and most dominant member of the pack, this alpha (for first) dog leads the pack in hunting, and therefore in surviving. This male will lead the pack away from danger, handle squabbles among pack members, and enforce pack rules. The alpha male gets his share of the "perks" of leadership.

BASSET ASSET

Bassets, as hunting hounds, fully grasp and expect a pack environment. Instead of several other dogs, you and your family must fill this pack role.

Some Bassets mature more quickly than others. Adjust your training to the level of maturity of your young Basset.

He eats first and is usually the sire of the puppies or cubs born to pack females.

The second dog in the pack is designated as the "beta" dog and so forth down the line until the very old dogs and puppies are included. Each animal has its place and knows it. This is the glue that holds the pack together. Without a pack, survival becomes much more difficult for wolves or wild dogs.

Your Basset will have a pack also. It consists of you and every other person in your household. It is crucial to understand that *every* human being *must* rank above the Basset in the pack. In the worst case a dog spots a vacuum in leadership at the alpha level and moves to fill it. In some breeds such a dog is truly dangerous as it will do only what it wants to do and will try to remain in the alpha position.

Your Basset is not an overly aggressive dog and battling for leadership isn't usually a Basset's style. The dog still needs to understand its place in the pack that lives at your house. It is natural for a lower member to obey the higher members in the pack. Your understanding of this truth and filling the role of the alpha male sets the stage for effective training for your Basset.

When to Start Training

Bassets are fairly slow to mature, with some maturing at different rates from others, even in the same litter. Some aspects of training have already begun for your Basset. It has learned to sleep by itself in its crate. It should also be house-trained. Depending on the level of maturity of

your puppy, more formal lessons can begin after the puppy is reasonably house-trained.

The Mother Dog as a Training Model

Even before you got your Basset puppy it had received some excellent training by one of the best trainers possible, its mother. In keeping with the pack concept and in keeping with the training tips, the mother is the leader of her pack of puppies. She enforces her will upon the baby Bassets even before they have been weaned. The mother dog uses several tried-and-true methods that are good models for you to follow in your training.

Repetition: The mother Basset made it clear to her puppies that some misbehaviors would not be allowed. Each time a puppy committed this misdeed, like straying too far away from the whelping box, the act was met with immediate correction. The mother Basset did this over and over until the puppies learned which behaviors got them punished.

Consistency: Already mentioned as a key, the mother dog is a perfect example of consistency. She didn't punish bad behavior one time and then reward it the next time. Her actions were identical each time.

Fairness: The mother Basset corrects her puppies fairly. She doesn't resort to physical violence in enforcing her will on the puppies. A rough nudge from Mama is all the puppies usually need to make them behave.

Follow this training model and you will find training your Basset is much less difficult because your puppy already knows how this model works.

Training Equipment

Several pieces of equipment will be needed for use in training your Basset.

1. You will need a chain training collar. This collar is different from your Basset's regular collar and should be used *only* for training purposes. When the young Basset sees this collar in your hand it should realize that training time is here.

This collar is often and falsely called a "choke" collar. Used correctly, this collar does not choke a dog. When you exert slight pressure on the lead (or leash) this chain collar causes the dog's head to be pulled up with a gentle tug. This is to get and maintain your Basset's attention so that it will be listening for the commands you are to give next. When used in conjunction with a firm (alpha male voice) "*No*" your Basset will know its actions are not to be repeated.

This chain collar should be large enough to go over your Basset's head and ears with no more than an inch (2.5 cm) clearance. This collar *must* be removed after each training session is over. This is the training collar that should signal an end to playtime and a beginning of training time. Its impact would be lost if it became an everyday collar. Additionally, leaving this chain collar on a dog could result in it snagging on something and either frightening the puppy or even possibly strangling the youngster.

2. You will also need a 1-inch (2.5-cm) wide lead or leash. This is a training lead and should not be used on regular walks and other outings. For a Basset this lead should be constructed of leather, nylon, or woven web material and it should be 6 feet (1.8 m) long. This training lead should have a comfortable hand loop on one end and a swivel snap, for attaching to the training collar, on the other end.

One trick used to help a young Basset get accustomed to the weight and pressure of the training collar and the training lead is to allow the youngster to run around (under close supervision) in a room or a backyard with the collar on and the lead dragging along behind. Supervision will prevent the lead from catching on something and frightening the young Basset.

It is important to successful training that the training collar and the training lead be associated in the dog's mind with the training classes. It is important that the Basset neither fear nor dislike either the collar or the lead.

Pretraining Hints

It is essential that you know how to correctly give the commands before you begin actual training:

1. Be firm: Give clear, one word commands to your puppy, using the dog's name before each command to get its attention:

"*Cleo, sit.*" Use an alpha voice; don't clutter the command with any other words. This is training time, not playtime.

2. Be consistent: Use the same tone of voice

each time, so that your puppy will know by the sound of your voice as well as by the actual command that you mean business.

3. Be specific: Don't string commands: "*Cleo, come here and sit down.*" Each command has a single, specific word. That word should be used each time in the same way to avoid confusing your Basset.

Your Basset will respond best if you have no hidden agendas that can creep into your voice. If you have had a bad day, don't try to train your dog. The tension in your voice will be conveyed to your puppy, who may believe it is at fault in some way. Training should be based on appropriate correction and praise, not on taking out one's hostilities on an innocent puppy.

4. Keep lessons brief, no more than 15 minutes. Teach one command at a time. Don't go on to another command until your puppy has mastered the previous command. It may take several months for your Basset to learn all of the commands, even longer in some cases. Let training be done in small, significant pieces rather than in a big, overdone, and usually fruitless manner.

When training time is over, don't immediately begin playing with your Basset puppy. Put the puppy back in its crate and wait 20 minutes. This will separate training time from playtime.

Other members of your household should understand that training your Basset puppy is important. They also need to understand the basics of each command so that they will not inadvertently undo your training when playing with the puppy.

Sitting is something that your Basset already knows how to do. As the trainer, your job is to teach your pet when and where to sit.

The Five Basic Commands

Sit

The *sit* is a good command on which to begin because your Basset already knows how to sit down. All you need to do is to teach the puppy to sit when and where you say.

1. Begin with your Basset wearing the training collar attached to the training lead.

2. Place the puppy on your *left* side next to your left leg. Hold the lead in your *right* hand.

3. In one *continuous* motion, gently pull the puppy's head *up,* as you push its hindquarters *down* with your left hand.

4. As you do this, give the firm command "*Sit.*"

When the puppy is in the sitting position, heap on the praise. Using the tip about continuous repetition, practice this command until your Basset will sit *without* having its rear pushed downward. (Remember the unique physique of the Basset and *never* force the

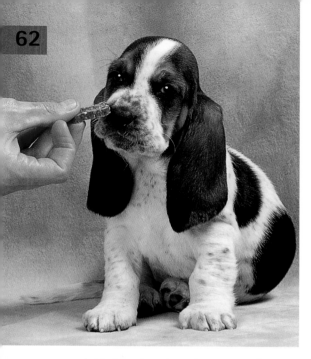

your Basset puppy in the sitting position on your *left* side. Initially you may use the lead to keep the puppy's head up, but the idea is to progress to a point where the lead isn't in your hand and you can walk away from the puppy.

1. Using your Basset's name, give the firm command "*Stay*."

2. As you give the command, step away from the dog (moving your *right* foot first), going forward.

3. At exactly the same time you are giving the command and stepping away, bring the palm of your *left* hand down in front of your Basset's face (*be careful not to unintentionally swat the dog on the nose*) in an upside-down version of the police hand signal for "*Stop*."

puppy's hindquarters down by overexerting pressure on its hindquarters! This could injure a young Basset.)

Keep training sessions on this command short. Don't leave the youngster in a *sit* long enough for the puppy to become bored. As it improves in following this command you can increase the length of time, always remembering to lavish praise on the Basset *each* time it does the *sit* correctly.

The *sit* is of great importance as it is the command from which most other commands are begun. Make certain that you take enough time with your Basset to ensure that it has mastered the *sit* before you move on to other commands.

Stay

Don't attempt the *stay* until your Basset does really well on the *sit*. Without the *sit* the *stay* cannot be taught. This command begins with

The stay is, at first, a bit difficult for some dogs, but persistence should make staying in one place (on command) something your Basset Hound will learn to do.

All three parts of the command, the verbal, the stepping away, and the hand signal *must* be done simultaneously and the same way *each* time. This command will really need consistent repetition because it goes against a strong urge the puppy has to move when you move. Don't expect long *stays* at the beginning. Praise the puppy for any length *stays*, but work to increase the time the dog remains seated.

If the puppy leaves the *stay* simply go back to the starting point, the sitting position on the left, and start all over again. Do this several times, carefully doing the same things in the same tone of voice each time. If your Basset puppy has some trouble with the *stay*, end each session with a few *sits* with the praise that goes with each *sit* so that your puppy can end each lesson on a positive note.

Once your puppy remains in a *stay* as you walk away, you can introduce the release word "*okay*," given in a cheerful, upbeat tone. This will allow the puppy to leave the *stay* and come to you to get his customary reward of hearty praise for remaining in the *stay*.

Teaching your Basset to heel will make walks much more pleasant. Rather than having your Basset lagging behind, charging ahead, or twisting the leash around your legs, a well-trained dog will walk in place beside you, with or without the leash.

Heel

Once the puppy has mastered the *sit* and the *stay* and feels comfortable with the training collar and training lead, you can start teaching the *heel*. Begin with your puppy in the *sit* position on your left.

1. Hold the lead in your *right* hand (controlling it with the left hand due to the shortness of the Basset).

2. Step out with your *left* foot.

3. Give the firm command "heel" as your puppy starts to walk with you. As in all commands, use the dog's name to begin the command: "*Cleo, heel.*"

If your Basset is inattentive or doesn't move out when you do, pop the slack of the lead loudly against the side of *your* leg (the equivalent of clapping your hands to get your puppy's attention), repeating the command, and walking away all in the same motion.

When the Basset puppy catches on to the fact that it should be walking along with you, give it some praise but do it as you walk along. Continue the praise as long as the Basset is

walking with you in the proper position on your left side.

When you stop, give the *sit* command. Once your Basset has mastered the *heel* it will sit automatically when you stop. Don't let the puppy lag behind you, get ahead of you, or twist around to the other side. The purpose of this command is to get the dog to not only walk with you, but to walk with you in the right place and stop and go as you do. Your ultimate goal in the *heel* is to be able to get your Basset to do it without the lead.

Never just drag your Basset along. If the youngster has trouble with the *heel*, go back to the sitting position and start all over again. Gentle tugs will get your Basset moving and keep him going. Eventually the *heel* will be a part of your Basset's command repertoire.

Down

The *down* begins in the *sit* and the *stay*. In the *down* you won't use the upward pull of these commands, which is designed to keep the puppy's head up. The *down* is a *stay* with the dog's belly resting on the ground or floor.

1. Pull *down* on the lead with your *right* hand.

2. Make a ball-bouncing-like, downward motion with your *left* palm to convey to your puppy the direction you want it to go.

3. As you pull down and give the downward hand signal give the firm command "*Down.*"

It is important that you don't use too much force to pull the Basset's chest downward. To do so could easily injure the puppy's frontquarters. As with all the commands, the physical steps and the verbal command must be given at exactly the same time so that the puppy makes the connection that the downward pressure,

the downward signal, and the command are all part of the same desired action on his part.

Once the puppy is down on its stomach, pour on the praise. Ultimately this command should be fairly easy for the Basset that doesn't have far to go to reach the required position. The goal is to have the puppy go into this position from the sit and then stay there until you release him to come to you.

Continue to practice the *down* with the *sit* and the *stay*. Consistency and persistency (through repetition) will usually teach a Basset to *down* and stay in that position.

Come

The *come* may seem like an easy command, but Bassets can sometimes be stubborn and may want to continue following some delicious smell they have discovered. There are several important elements to the *come* that aren't as necessary in the other basics. Rather than concentrating on your firm, authoritarian, alpha voice, let your genuine enthusiasm for the puppy show through as you give the command "*Come.*"

Your Basset will probably want to be with you and so this command is calling for the puppy to do what he wants to do anyway. It is important to make the *come* something the puppy will obey *immediately*, as his life may someday depend on it!

At the beginning you may want to use your regular training lead, switching to a longer lead, one of 20 feet (6 m) or so to reinforce the idea that the command, "*Cleo, Come*" means now, no matter how far away the puppy may be. You can gradually, gently but firmly, tug on the lead to start the puppy in your direction while you give the command.

Your Basset will benefit from outings with other dog owners, such as obedience classes and dog parks.

The *come* is also different from the other commands in that it shouldn't be repeated over and over again in each session. Even with a praise reward each rime the puppy obeys, a Basset can become tired of continually being called to you over a short span of time. Use the *come* unexpectedly in play sessions or when the Basset is just walking around in the backyard. Always expect immediate obedience just as the puppy should always expect to be praised for obeying.

Note: A *very* important aspect of this command concerns *when* you call your Basset and for *what* reasons. *Never* call your dog to you for something that the dog views as unpleasant. This includes scolding, baths (if the dog doesn't like them), and other negatives. Using this important command under these circumstances can be counterproductive. The *come* should be viewed by the puppy as a happy reuniting with the human it loves so much. Consistency in the use of this command is crucial. If a Basset responds appropriately to your command it should expect its customary reward, *not* a reprimand. If you have to correct the dog or do something that it doesn't like, *you go to the dog*! Don't ruin a good command by creating

ambivalence in the dog's mind as to whether the *come* command should be obeyed.

Obedience Classes

If you have never trained a dog before, you may discover that you and your Basset can get a great deal of assistance by attending local dog training classes. Not only are these classes usually taught by real training experts, they will give you a chance to mingle with other dog owners who are pretty much in the same position you are in. Your Basset can become a little more socialized to other people and other dogs. You may be able to find out information about veterinarians, new products, foods, and other things you would otherwise miss out on.

If you have developed some friendships with more experienced Basset people, ask them about which training classes they may recommend. Specific training questions or problems could also be mentioned to these breed experts who may have an answer for you.

BASSET ASSET

Bassets and their owners may require some additional training expertise. In most communities there are dog trainers or training clubs that help.

YOUR BASSET AS A FIELD TRIAL OR HUNTING DOG

Heralding a hunting heritage, the Basset Hound remains one of the best of the basic hound types. Originally bred to pursue rabbits and hares in a slow and deliberate manner, the Basset still fulfills this function today. Some hunters still go afield with their Bassets. The American Kennel Club and other organizations have codified rules and procedures for hunting field trials.

Not only does this versatile breed have what it takes to be an excellent companion and pet, win in tough competition in the conformation show ring, show its smarts and training by capturing sought-after obedience titles, the Basset can also be a more than competent field trial and hunting dog. Some people forget this breed was a widely acknowledged hunting hound for centuries before it won hearts as a pet and companion, won ribbons in the show ring, and won titles for its obedience work!

The Basset Hound is still an able competitor in the ages-old sport of tracking rabbits and

Hunting and field trials are excellent ways of channeling your Basset's abilities.

hares. While the Beagle also has a great following in this popular endeavor, the Basset has many admirers among the field trial set. Usually slower than the Beagle or Harrier (a breed of hound between the Beagle and Foxhound in size), the endurance and excellent scenting ability of the Basset give it an edge in events where the winner needs staying power!

Basset Hound field trials are regulated by several national dog organizations, the largest being the American Kennel Club (AKC). Trials are run in a variety of ways: with braces of two dogs, small packs, and large packs of Bassets pursuing the wily rabbit through its natural habitat. Licensed field trial judges follow along,

observing, evaluating the performance of each dog, and selecting the winning dog at trial's end. Trophies, fame, championship points, and acclaim from other field trialers are among the hard-sought prizes.

Bassets are also used as rabbit hunting dogs. Because of their slower speed and more deliberate style, Bassets still have their advocates among hunters who want to be able to keep up with the dogs. Bassets, and Basset-crosses, have been used in a variety of other game from pheasants to deer. In each instance the scenting ability and the endurance of the Basset have been among the attributes the hunters sought in their dogs.

In hunting and field trial events, the Basset also brings another, more aesthetic quality. Bas-

sets have some of the most wonderful hound voices in all of dogdom! Their baying, especially in a pack, or on a track, is music to the ears of both experienced and neophyte hound admirers alike. Much like the voice of the large Bloodhound, the voice of the Basset has a ring of its own that evokes visions of the centuries of this short hound's close association as a hunting companion for the gentry in France, England, and the early United States.

A Matter of Your Basset's Heritage

Bassets have been used as hunting hounds for hundreds of years. They were especially developed for this purpose and many Bassets, even some AKC champions, can still handle field work very well.

Hunting with Your Basset

Using your Basset as a hunting dog will allow you and the dog some exercise. Be sure that you are fully licensed as a hunter, that your Basset has all its immunizations, and that the place where you are hunting is open land or that you have permission to hunt there.

Rabbit hunting generally allows one or more dogs to pick up the scent of the game, follow the game, and then turn the game so that it will run back past where you are waiting.

Bassets do this very well. Unless you are an experienced hunter, go with someone who you feel is at ease in this environment.

Be careful with your firearms and be certain of what you are shooting. More than one novice hunter, shooting at the first sound he hears, has wounded or killed his dog.

Added Care for a Field Dog

Field work exposes your Basset to scratches, cuts, and abrasions that dogs don't get in their backyards. Be sure to carefully go over the Basset, after you have returned home, for any injuries or parasites (see Ticks, page 87). Give special attention to the dog's underside, ears, and eyes.

A hardworking field dog may need added nutrition if hunting is a common occurrence for you and your Basset. You should also carry some drinking water to the field with you and a dish from which the Basset can drink.

Large Packs

There are several kennels in the United States and other countries that regularly go to the field with large packs of Bassets. This is an exciting event to see. Some hunts of this sort are by invitation only, but others will allow visitors.

Field Trialing with Your Basset

The American Kennel Club (AKC) has established a set of rules that pertain to Bassets and field trials. Field trails are not for hunting rabbits, they are for grading a dog's capacity to track a rabbit. Many times Basset events are held in large enclosures used for Beagle field trials. These enclosures, often called running grounds, may be 20 or 30 acres inside of a

sturdy fence designed to keep four-footed predators out and away from the population of rabbits that is maintained in each running ground.

A large group of bystanders will begin to march in a line through the running grounds, which are allowed to have high weeds and tall grass to make rabbits safe from owls and hawks. This line continues to go forward until a rabbit jumps up and starts running. The person who spotted the rabbit yells "Tally-Ho."

The spotter then points to the last place the rabbit was seen. Two or three Bassets are brought to this spot and allowed to nose around until they pick up the rabbit's scent. When they have it they are released from their leads and judges walk along behind them assessing how faithful each dog is to following the exact trail that the rabbit took.

Deductions are made when a dog loses the scent, has to backtrack, or gets on another scent. The Basset with the least amount of mistakes is the winner of this particular run. If its score is high enough this Basset may be brought back to compete for the winner of the trial, second place, third place, fourth place, and NBQ (Next Best Qualified).

While there are still, as yet, fewer Basset trials, field trialing with Beagles is one of the largest dog-participation activities in the United States. Basset trials are growing in number and afford some excellent fun for a dog and a dog owner.

BASSET ASSET
Bassets come by their scenting ability honestly. The cute Basset that you so love as a pet is descended from countless generations of highly valued hunting dogs.

FEEDING YOUR BASSET

All dogs need the right foods on which to thrive. Without the right foods many dogs just never reach their genetic potential. As important as any aspect of dog care, feeding is one of the most misunderstood and neglected subjects. There are many viewpoints about which dog food is best, but all animal nutritionists acknowledge that a balanced diet is always the right thing for your dog.

The Importance of a Good Diet

In addition to balanced nutrition, there are three primary rules to follow in feeding your dog:

1. Find a high-quality, nutritionally complete dog food and feed it *consistently.*

2. Don't feed more than your pet really needs, even if he wants more.

3. Never feed table scraps, either mixed with regular dog food or as treats.

The Elements of a Balanced Diet

A balanced, nutritionally complete diet for dogs is composed of seven key elements: proteins, carbohydrates, fats, vitamins, minerals, good drinking water, and the knowledge and level of feeding consistency of the dog owner.

Proteins

Proteins provide your Basset Hound with the essential amino acids needed for growth, development of strong bones (so important to Basset Hounds) and muscles and the continued health of these bones and muscles, and the healing of injured bones and muscles.

Proteins also promote the production of antibodies that help in fighting infection throughout the dog's entire body. Additionally, proteins are important in the production of enzymes and hormones so necessary for the ongoing chemical processes occurring inside your Basset.

Carbohydrates

Carbohydrates and fats are the primary energy sources that keep dogs going. Carbohydrates are not as concentrated an energy source as are fats, but they are still a crucial part of the balanced canine diet.

Carbohydrates provide about half the energy as the same amount of fats would. For older dogs and breeds like the Basset, that can easily become obese, carbohydrates are often used for lowered fat diets.

Fats

Not only do fats in a diet provide double the energy of carbohydrates, fats also serve an important delivery service. It is through fats that the fat-soluble vitamins, A, D, E, and K, are made available to your Basset's system. Fats also help keep coats shiny and skin healthy.

Fats also play an important role in many dog foods. Fats make dog foods taste better. Foods that taste better (the concept is called palatability) are more likely to be eaten than are foods without sufficient fat content.

Vitamins

Another food-related area filled with misunderstanding concerns the need for vitamins for dogs. Many people are so accustomed to taking vitamins that they assume their dog should be on a vitamin program too. This is usually unnecessary, and it can be harmful.

Modern premium dog foods are balanced. They include all the vitamins that dogs will need. The best way to provide vitamins for your Basset Hound is to find the right food and feed it consistently. Unless your Basset-knowledgeable veterinarian urges you to give vitamins to your Basset, leave them alone.

Minerals

As is the case with vitamins, minerals can be easily overdone. Bassets have unique needs, needs that can be both met and worsened by supplementation. Discuss minerals with your friends who are Basset experts and with your Basset-knowledgeable veterinarian. Most nutritionally complete and balanced dog foods are sufficient in the minerals dogs need. Unless you are given sound, expert advice to the contrary, leave minerals, like vitamins, alone.

Water

One of the most important parts of good nutrition is plenty of pure, fresh drinking water. Water not only quenches a Basset's thirst, it also plays a key role in respiration and in keeping the Basset's system at safe temperature levels.

Clean water bowls regularly and keep them full of fresh, cool water. You wouldn't want to drink out of a foul-smelling, algae-ridden, slimy water bowl; neither does your Basset Hound. When water is hot from sun exposure, dirty, or stale, dogs may not drink enough of it. Your Basset can live a lot longer without food than it can without water.

Owner Knowledge and Consistency

Many dog owners don't consider what foods their dogs eat to be very important. They buy whatever product is on sale or whatever strikes their interest at a particular moment. Many people know more about cute dog food ads than they do about the dog foods these ads sell.

Without a quality food, a dog simply will not reach its potential. Poor-quality, generic-type dog foods are made with less attention to the nutritional balance than to the bank balance. Cheap foods are made of cheap ingredients; they are processed in cheap ways, using cheap equipment. The result of such food being fed to a Basset Hound can be nothing else but cheap.

Dog owners need to know what goes into the foods their dog eats. They need to observe dog stools, which are a sure indicator of dog food quality (better foods are more digestible and the stools are generally smaller and firmer).

Dog owners need to find a really good food and stay with it.

The best dog foods in the world won't work the way they are designed to if the person feeding them is inconsistent. The number of feedings, the amount of food per feeding, and the overall appearance of the dog while on a specific food, should all be factored in by an aware dog owner.

Special Basset Hound Dietary Concerns

Because they are the only large, short-legged dogs, Bassets need special attention paid to their feeding. It is quite easy to overfeed a Basset. Their appetites are generally very good and their sad expressions can practically beg for just a little more food in the food bowl. Nevertheless obesity is one of the biggest killers of dogs. In Bassets they are not only killed by obesity, but they are crippled by the effects of too much weight on the elongated spines and on their hearts.

Bassets have a huge bone structure. They need a nutritionally complete and balanced diet to develop these bones. Too little quality nutrition can leave a Basset spindly and unable to support its own weight. Too much nutrition can make a Basset fat and lead to a host of problems. Talk with experienced Basset breeders and Basset-knowledgeable veterinarians about approaches they have taken in walking the line between too much food and not enough food.

Commercial Dog Foods

There are three main kinds of commercial dog foods: canned, dry, and semimoist. Each kind has certain advantages.

Canned

Canned dog food is the most palatable form of dog food. It is also the most expensive, most likely to produce loose and smelly stools, and most likely to promote obesity when it is overused.

Canned foods, sometimes referred to as wet dog foods, are usually quite meaty and aromatic. This enhances their palatability. If a dog is started on canned food it is very difficult to ever get that dog to easily accept dry or semimoist foods.

Canned foods, which are from 75 to 85 percent moisture, can quickly spoil even at room temperature. Dogs fed exclusively on canned foods, which are softer than dry and somewhat softer than semimoist, tend to have more dental problems than dogs fed on crunchier foods, especially dry foods.

Canned dog foods have excellent shelf life if left unopened. They are convenient in cans that can serve as one meal for a dog. They store better in a dog owner's home than dry foods. They can be used as mixers with dry foods to improve palatability.

Dry

Dry dog foods are the most popular of the premium dog foods. They are also quite cost-effective, a point not lost on Basset owners. They have the best digestibility rates of any dog foods and, because of this, they make kennel cleanup much easier.

Dry foods can make staving off obesity easier for Basset owners because dry food can be fed in increasingly smaller portions of less nutritional concentration than canned and semimoist. Dry foods also keep well after being opened.

Palatability of many dry foods, which have a moisture rating of about 10 percent, isn't as good as for canned and semimoist. Premium dry foods have made great strides in solving this taste problem. Dry foods have a lot of versatility. They can easily be mixed with other dry foods when changing from one food to another as desired. Dry foods can be moistened if need be, but canned foods cannot usually be dried out.

Dry food manufacturers point out that dry products with their crunchier form will help scrape tartar off a dog's teeth. While this is true as far as it goes, no dry food should replace a regular dental care plan for your Basset.

Scrap the Table Scraps

Table scraps are completely unacceptable for Basset Hounds. Bassets, possibly more than any other breed, need a well balanced, nutritionally complete diet to avoid the crippling

Table scraps are the greatest contributor to life-threatening obesity in dogs. As a breed, the Basset suffers greatly from being overweight. No table scraps ever!

side effects of being overweight. Table scraps throw off the balance of a dog's diet and because they are generally eaten with great vigor, these leftovers may cause a Basset not to eat enough of its own dog food. Nutritionally, deficiencies could result.

Feeding Bassets at Different Ages

Feeding young Bassets is a fairly complex matter. You have to provide enough nutrition for them to grow their massive bones and large-size bodies. You must also feed carefully enough so that the size of the puppy doesn't grow faster than the capacity of its still pliable bones to support the weight. Rapid growth rates can result in developmental bone diseases.

There are a number of premium puppy foods available now that can help Bassets grow, but do so at a rate that fits their skeletal development

Feeding Basset puppies is very important. It is advisable for any first-time Basset owner to discuss feeding for Bassets of all ages with experienced Basset breeders, but especially the feeding of Basset puppies during their formative time. Veterinarians that are familiar with

the special needs of Basset Hounds may be able to recommend appropriate puppy foods.

Puppies should be fed four to six times each day. They should be fed only what they can finish during these mealtimes. Several feedings are always preferable to one or two large feedings. House-training is also much easier if you are controlling the puppy's food intake.

Feed the same food that the breeder of your puppy was feeding. This will avoid the nutritional and gastrointestinal trauma that most dogs and puppies have when their diets are abruptly changed. Unless the breeder has been having problems with the ration she has been feeding, or if you can't get this food in your area, stick with the same food as long as it matches the needs of your Basset puppy.

When Basset Hounds have reached maturity their nutritional needs become somewhat different from those of rapidly growing puppies. Mature adults should be able to utilize what they eat and not begin to get fat. Some strains (families) of Bassets may be more prone to obesity than others. Gauge how you feed adults by the specific needs of your Basset and on the wise counsel of the breeder from whom you bought the dog.

Adult dogs can get by with two feedings per day. These feedings should be as consistent as possible as to time, amount, place (within the home), and certainly the brand of food used.

As with puppies, don't change brands of dog foods just to try something new.

Some Bassets may mature more slowly than others. If your Basset still appears to be devel-

oping at two years old, don't let some arbitrary number cause you to move a still-growing Basset onto the adult Basset plateau.

If your adult Basset is a breeding animal, a show or obedience trial dog, or a hunting hound, the stresses and exercise of these endeavors may call for a little more nutrition, but even for active Bassets, don't overdo it with food.

Feeding Older Bassets

Older Bassets are the ones that usually start putting on weight. Feeding these older dogs takes a great deal of attention to their needs

and to preventing obesity. As dogs get older their metabolisms begin to slow down. They do less, therefore they need less food.

BASSET ASSET

Bassets don't need leftover human food in the form of table scraps (no matter how much they may like them). They need a good age-related diet designed specifically for canines.

This is the age group that some Basset owners begin to "kill with kindness." They just can't resist giving the old dog some morsel from the dinner table, or perhaps a little more dog food. Dog owners have been known to illogically say, "I always feed Cleo a full bowl of dog food and have since she was a puppy."

Unless you show real restraint in feeding an older Basset the risk is very great that obesity will become a problem with your dog. This is a terrible way for an older dog to have to exist. The added weight puts stress, sometimes great stress, on the old dog's spine, joints, and heart. Obesity is preventable, but only if the dog owners prevent it.

Many premium dog food companies now make foods designed specifically for older dogs. Many of these are nutritionally balanced foods that have less fat than foods for younger dogs. Your Basset breeder friends and your veterinarian can help you discover which of these brands might be right for your older Basset.

Feeding Spayed and Neutered Basset Hounds

Bassets that have no future as breeding stock or show dogs should be spayed or neutered. Feeding spays and neuters is much like feeding older Bassets. The accent is on preventing obesity by feeding a little less and walking a little longer for exercise. The same foods that are designed for adult or senior age dogs can also serve the spayed and neutered Bassets.

Treats

Everyone likes to give his or her dog a treat now and then. Unfortunately, many treat items can upset the balance of a dog's diet. Some dog food manufacturers are now making dog biscuits that match the formulas of their various foods for different age dogs. These treats, given in moderation, should neither throw off the dog food's balance nor contribute significantly to obesity.

It is so easy to overdo treats. One Basset Hound owner noticed her older dog gaining weight. She immediately found a lower-calorie food and began feeding that. Months later the Basset was still getting fat. The owner discovered that each member of her family had fallen for the "Great Basset Scam" and had given the sad-looking oldster a treat every day, certain that one treat wouldn't hurt. Unfortunately, there were five members in this family, which meant five treats each day!

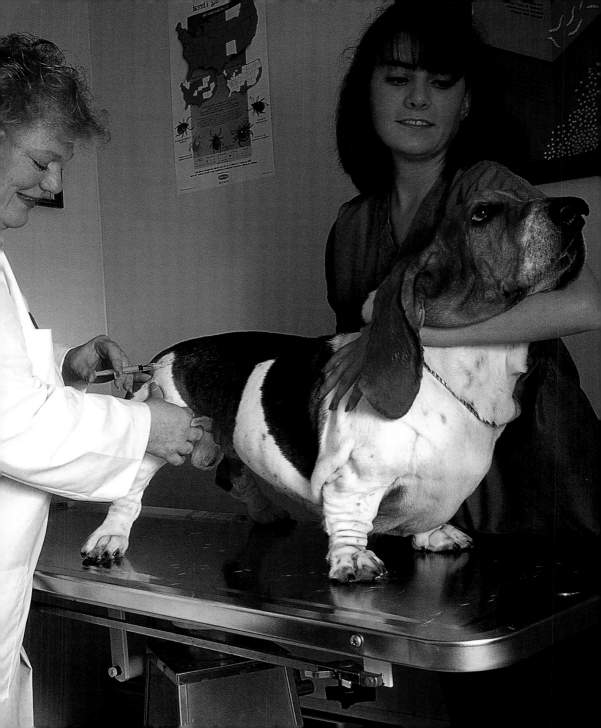

KEEPING YOUR BASSET HOUND HEALTHY

Any time the form of a breed has moved too far from the natural wolf structure, breeds will have problems. The Basset is just about as far from the wolf structure as any breed can be, yet in spite of its identification as a chondrodystrophiod breed, which refers to the unique Basset appearance, Bassets have relatively few inherited defects or physical problems. Some breeds have many more genetically determined concerns than do the Bassets.

Special Health Concerns for Basset Hounds

Obesity

That great killer of dogs of most breeds, obesity is the great crippler of long-bodied dogs such as the Basset. Their long spines just can't handle the strain of all that added weight. Proper feeding

Bassets need regular medical care from puppyhood through old age. Provide this care and your Basset Hound will be with you for many years.

and exercise can help forestall or even eliminate obesity as a problem for your Basset.

Von Willebrand's Disease

This inherited blood disorder is observed in as many as 15 percent of Bassets. This hemophilia-like ailment stems from an abnormality in the platelets in a dog's blood, which causes moderate to severe free bleeding.

Glaucoma

Bassets as a breed seem to be genetically predisposed to glaucoma. Clinical signs are painful, bulging eyes. Other eye problems for

Bassets include entropion (inversion or turning in of the eyelids) and ectropion (excessively droopy lower eyelids).

Paneosteitis

Also known as transient lameness or wandering lameness, paneosteitis is an inflammation of the long bones in dogs from six months to two years of age. Thought to be worsened by stress, many young dogs (as do youngsters of other breeds with similar problems) simply outgrow it. Unfortunately, paneosteitis is sometimes misdiagnosed and surgery has been performed when the ailment is usually short-termed.

Paneosteitis is one of the reasons that experienced Basset breeders don't encourage much exercise in very young Bassets. Exercise can aggravate this condition and make it appear worse than it really is.

Allergies

Some Bassets have a number of allergies, dermatitis, and seborrhea. The deep facial wrinkles cause these conditions to worsen. The Basset's long ears are also subject to skin problems and should be examined regularly and thoroughly cleaned with a mild cleanser.

Feet Problems

Not only are there possible skeletal problems in overweight Bassets, but they are prone to interdigital (between the toes) infections and cysts.

Breeding Difficulties

Their unique physiques make natural mating difficult for most Bassets and impossible for some. Hand-mating methods, where both the stud and the bitch are held in place for a mat-

BASSET ASSET
Bassets need regularly scheduled (and kept) veterinary appointments. Preventive care (immunizations) and overall checkups are crucial for health and long life.

ing, are practiced by many experienced Basset breeders.

Preventing Health Problems

Your Basset Hound will depend on you for everything in its life: food, lodging, training, and other essentials. One of the most important areas of responsibility you have is the health of your Basset. Because of the Basset's unusual physical structure, a large dog on very short legs, a greater responsibility falls on you. A medium-sized dog with average-length legs will have enough problems, but a dog with a very long spine, an atypical canine front end, and the bad habit of wandering away from home will bring new challenges.

Preventing health problems is far better than treating health problem. The problem of the wandering Basset can be stopped with good fences and better supervision. The spine and other Basset characteristics will need attention to many aspects of Basset life. Avoiding obesity in your Basset can certainly not hurt the spine. Being certain that puppies don't injure themselves by ascending or descending stairs and steps is another way. Buying a good puppy from a kennel known for few genetic defects and inheritable problems is another way to insure that your Basset will have a better chance at staying healthy.

A good, regular relationship with a veterinarian who has some understanding of the special problems of Bassets will be a key part of your plan to prevent health problems. Experienced Basset breeders who have "been there and done that" with Bassets can share their own health care plans and even help you develop yours.

✔ Keep your Basset from preventable harm.

✔ Handle medical problems by taking serious concerns immediately to the veterinarian. Feed wisely and never overfeed.

✔ Read everything available to you about special Basset maladies.

✔ Train your family to look out for the best interests of the health and safety of this shortest member of your family.

Immunize Against Diseases

Veterinary medicine has come a long way in the past several decades. Diseases that once wiped out entire kennels are now rarely, if ever, seen in the United States. Today's Basset has the best chance of going through its life without a serious illness as any Basset has ever had. A solid immunization program, in the hands of skilled veterinarians, has made the expectation of a longer life for your Basset very much a reality.

The first immunizations your Basset should receive include distemper, parvovirus, hepatitis, leptospirosis, parainfluenza, and coronavirus. Your Basset puppy should have received these shots at six weeks, others at eight weeks, and still others at twelve weeks.

Distemper

Distemper was once the greatest known threat to puppies and young dogs. Great kennels sometimes simply ceased to exist following a severe outbreak of distemper.

The immunization for distemper has struck a mighty blow in decreasing the incidence of this killer disease. Although still deadly in places without immunizations and in wild canine populations, distemper has been much less in evidence in recent decades.

Distemper is characterized by clinical signs that may appear as soon as a week after an unimmunized dog has come into contact with an animal with distemper. At first, distemper may look like a cold and a runny nose and a slight fever. Dogs with distemper will usually stop eating, become fatigued, listless, and suffer from diarrhea. Rush a puppy with these clinical signs to the veterinarian!

Rabies

At one time stories of rabid animals roaming the countryside were the basis for many nightmares. The same thing is true today in many places in the world, and in some places in the United States. Rabies became all the more frightening because it could be transferred to humans by a once-loving family dog.

Rabies can afflict any warm-blooded mammal and is passed on through saliva usually conveyed by a bite. In some parts of this country rabies is still widespread among some populations of wild animals: foxes, raccoons, and others. An unimmunized dog that comes in contact with an animal with rabies can contract and spread the disease itself.

There are two forms of rabies: "furious" and "dumb." In the furious form the classical "mad dog" behavior is observed in which an afflicted animal charges about biting anything and everything that it can get to, even trees or automobiles. Dumb rabies causes the animal to be almost sedentary with paralysis, unconsciousness, and finally death. Some victims of furious rabies die while in the furious stage. Others go into the dumb stage and die.

Failure to keep your Basset immunized against rabies is both negligent and unlawful. Make certain that rabies isn't one of the medical problems you have to be concerned about with your Basset!

Leptospirosis

Leptospirosis is a bacterial disease that primarily damages the kidneys of a dog with the disease. In advanced cases, leptospirosis can also do harm to a dog's liver, which can produce mouth sores, jaundice, weight loss, and weakness in the dog's hindquarters.

Spread primarily by water contaminated by an animal with the disease, leptospirosis has several clinical signs: loss of appetite, fever, diarrhea, abdominal pain, and vomiting. Immunization and annual booster shots thereafter will keep leptospirosis away from your Basset Hound.

Hepatitis

Infectious canine hepatitis is not the same disease afflicting humans. The canine form can affect any canine and can go from being a mild infection to a deadly bout with the disease that can kill a dog within one day after it is diagnosed.

Spread by contact with the urine or feces of an affected animal, infectious canine hepatitis shows clinical signs that include listlessness, abdominal pain, tonsillitis, light sensitivity, fever, and bloody diarrhea or vomiting.

Annual boosters following an initial immunization will protect your dog from hepatitis.

Parvovirus

Young puppies are often the victims of parvovirus, but this viral disease can kill any unprotected dog at any age! This killer usually attacks a dog or puppy's immune system, gastrointestinal tract, heart, and bone marrow. Puppies often suffer from severe dehydration due to heavy vomiting and thin and bloody diarrhea. In 48 hours from the onset of the disease, parvovirus can claim the life of its victim.

Immediate medical care can save some puppies with parvovirus. An effective immunization program can save even more puppies from this virus.

Parainfluenza

Parainfluenza is thought to be spread by *both* contact with an infected animal and by particles expelled in breathing and coughing from dogs with parainfluenza. Parainfluenza is highly contagious and can spread rapidly through an entire kennel, affecting all unimmunized dogs there.

Parainfluenza can be a cause of tracheobronchitis (with its dry, hacking cough and repeated efforts by the sick dog to cough up mucus). Not usually a killer in and of itself, parainfluenza seriously weakens its victims to such an extent that they may fall prey to other infections and diseases.

Parainfluenza can bring on tracheobronchitis. Tracheobronchitis often has a fellow traveler, *bordetella*, which is the most common bacteria isolated from dogs that have tracheobronchitis. This sidekick ailment generally is found in tracheobronchitis' most serious form, bacterial bronchopneumonia.

This whole group of intertwined illnesses can be prevented by immunization.

Coronavirus

Dogs of all ages can contract coronavirus, which is highly contagious. Clinical signs of this disease are soft or even runny stools up to very foul-smelling and watery diarrhea. Other signs include vomiting. While treatment can save a victim of coronavirus, the dog or puppy is often left in a greatly weakened condition and open to other infections.

Borelliosis (Lyme Disease)

This tick-borne disease affects many mammals, including human beings. Medically termed borelliosis, Lyme disease in humans is now called Lyme Arthritis. This is a serious and potentially fatal (more to you than to your dog) illness spread by the tiny deer tick (and possibly other ticks). Dogs and humans have come into contact with this ailment by being in tick-infested areas.

First diagnosed in Lyme, Connecticut, borelliosis is now found in every part of the United States. Once viewed as only a hunters' disease, borelliosis now has surfaced in city parks and other urban recreation areas, places where you and your Basset Hound might go.

Clinical signs of Lyme disease include tenderness around joints accompanied by swelling, and loss of appetite. If a tick bites you or your Basset, or you find a tick in your clothing but no evident bite, seek immediate medical care. Have all ticks checked out by trained personnel. This is an ailment that can kill you. Take no chances with any ticks.

Other Medical Conditions, Illnesses, and Concerns

Diarrhea

Some diarrhea is common in dogs and puppies. It may be caused by changes in diet, stress, or by internal parasites. Diarrhea can also be a danger signal of the onset of a serious illness. Diarrhea that continues beyond 24 hours merits a trip to the veterinarian for you and your Basset. As an aside, have your veterinarian check your Basset's anal glands.

Vomiting

Like diarrhea, some vomiting is to be expected. Excitement can bring on vomiting in a young puppy. Like diarrhea, food changes and stress can also cause vomiting.

It is also true of vomiting that it may be the first indicator of a more serious problem. Together, diarrhea and vomiting can quickly

lead to dehydration, a serious condition in a puppy. Vomiting more than 3 times in a 24-hour period warrants a veterinary visit.

Parasites

External Parasites

Fleas: Fleas have always plagued dogs. They are the most common parasite affecting dogs and they actually survive by feeding on the dog's blood. In severe infestations, fleas can cause anemia and possibly fatal conditions for very young puppies.

These parasites have a parasite of their own which they pass on to their host—the dog. Tapeworms get into a dog's system through fleas. Some dogs, like some people, have severe allergic reactions to flea bites. This flea bite allergy can cause severe scratching, hair loss, and great discomfort for the allergic dog. This allergic reaction requires immediate treatment by a veterinarian.

A flea infestation means going to war against these parasites to get rid of them. This war must be fought on every front; anywhere that your Basset can go can have fleas—your home, your yard, the doghouse and kennel, your car, your summer cottage, and anywhere you went with your dog. Fleas leave multitudes of eggs everywhere that they can get to. Killing just

Fleas can carry a parasite of their own— the tapeworm—that is passed on when a flea-infested Basset chews at and then swallows a flea. Bad enough on their own, fleas add to a dog's health problems by being an agent of tapeworms.

the fleas on the dog is pointless if the dog is returned to an environment loaded with newly hatched fleas.

Consult your veterinarian or a pet products professional about the arsenal of anti-flea weapons you will need in this war. Flea dips, flea shampoos, flea collars, flea dust, and similar products are all designed for use on the dog. Foggers, carpet sprays, and cleaners are for your home. Yard spray and kennel dust is designed to get those fleas that live outside.

Fleas spend 90 percent of their life cycle *off* the dog. Only the adult fleas, about 10 percent of the total flea population, are actually on your Basset.

Ticks: Ticks are larger parasites than fleas, but they are easier to kill. Ticks gorge themselves on your dog's blood (or your blood) and greatly expand in size. Their bites are not only unsightly but can become infected and cause more serious conditions. Some ticks even carry potentially deadly diseases such as Lyme disease (see Borelliosis, page 85) or Rocky Mountain Spotted fever, both of which can affect dogs and humans.

Ticks can usually be eliminated with regular use of veterinarian-recommended sprays, dips, powders, and flea and tick collars. Your home and yard can be sprayed either by you or by an exterminator.

Ear mites: Your Basset has long, hanging ears that create great hiding places for the pesky ear mite. These microscopic pests live in both the ear and the ear canal. You know ear mites are there when you see their dirty-looking, waxy, dark residue on the skin inside the ear.

Ear mites can make your Basset very uncomfortable. If you see your dog violently shaking his head from side to side, or if the dog contin-ually digs at or scratches at his ears, ear mites are the usual cause. See your veterinarian about how to handle these bothersome parasites.

Mange: There are two kinds of mange, both of which are caused by mites:
• **Demodectic**, or what was once called "red" mange, is a problem for both very young and very old dogs. Demodectic mange causes rough and patchy-looking places around a dog or puppy's head, face, eyes, and throat. This mange can also cause widespread hair loss, and often quite painful itching.
• **Sarcoptic** mange is caused by a different mite from the mite that causes demodectic mange. The sarcoptic mange mite burrows into the skin. It can cause severe hair loss and itching that can make an afflicted dog scratch himself until he bleeds. Transferable to humans, sarcoptic mange is usually short-lived on people, but it can cause a rash and some itching.

Consult with your veterinarian about what remedies are available to treat and prevent a recurrence of both kinds of mange.

Internal Parasites
• **Roundworms:** Roundworms attack the health and vitality of dogs of all ages. These parasites are especially tough on young puppies that may have gotten infested by roundworms through their mother, even before they were born. If the mother has roundworms she will pass them on, which is a good reason for having all brood bitches dewormed before they are bred.

Roundworms do much to sap the health away from infested animals. Basset puppies that have a lot of growing to do in a short time don't need this further drag on their strength and ability to grow up healthy.

Mosquitos pass on heartworm larvae from other animals already infected with heartworms. Untreated, these larvae mature and can literally clog a dog's heart, producing great suffering and eventual death.

Your veterinarian will be able to rid dogs and puppies of roundworms, but you need to keep your kennel and surrounding area as clean as possible to avoid reinfestation. Remember that roundworms can also infest human beings!

• **Hookworms:** Hookworms can infest dogs of all ages, but growing puppies are especially vulnerable to these little worms that are much like lamprey eels in that they attach themselves to the sides of a puppy's small intestine and drain off blood. Hookworms generally weaken a puppy's ability to fight off infections and diseases.

Clinical signs of hookworms include bloody, tarlike stools. This parasite is definitely an immediate job for your veterinarian.

• **Tapeworms:** Fleas introduce tapeworm larvae into a dog's system. Tapeworms aren't as life-robbing as some other worms, but they need to be eradicated by your veterinarian. Tapeworms can sometime grow quite long inside a host animal; segments of tapeworms are sometimes seen in the stools of an infested animal.

• **Heartworms:** Among the most dangerous internal parasites is the heartworm. Once a problem confined to the southern United States, heartworms now are found in much of the country.

The heartworm gains access into the dog's bloodstream through the bite of a mosquito that is a heartworm carrier. Once inside your Basset Hound, heartworm larvae begin to move toward the dog's heart. Unless they are eradicated, heartworms will ultimately clog the heart and kill the infested pet.

There are heartworm preventive medicines that must be started *before* a dog has heartworm larvae actually in his bloodstream. After a dog is infested a serious, and potentially dangerous, treatment program must be undertaken to get rid of the heartworms. The uninfested animal can now be given the preventive medicine.

Emergency Care for Your Basset Hound

If your Basset should be injured there are some things you can do to help the dog and not make matters worse:

✔ Remain calm. Dogs can always pick up heightened anxiety levels from their owners.

✔ Talk to the Basset in calm, reassuring words, showing your confidence and radiating that confidence to your dog that you will make everything all right.

✔ Move slowly with no sudden motions or gestures that could alarm an already injured and frightened pet.

✔ Regardless of whether this dog is yours and has never tried to bite anyone, gently put a muzzle on the dog as a safety precaution. If a muzzle isn't available a necktie, a belt, even a scarf can handle the job. Use caution with a muzzle on a dog that has been vomiting to protect against choking.

✔ After muzzling is completed, stop any bleeding immediately by pressure or by tourniquets.

✔ Move an injured dog *very* carefully in order to not make the injuries worse or hurt the dog unnecessarily. If you can get some help, use a table or a door or something sturdy to help you transport a heavy Basset Hound.

✔ If you have no help, maneuver the injured dog onto a tarpaulin, a blanket, or even a small rug. Slowly and gently drag this makeshift stretcher along to transportation to the veterinarian.

✔ Call your veterinarian on your cell phone or have someone else call to alert him or her of your impending arrival and the nature of the injuries, if possible.

BASSET ASSET

Bassets have several ongoing health concerns that you should learn about and know how to spot in your own Basset should the situation arise.

✔ Drive safely and sanely to the veterinarian's office and avoid putting an injured pet through two accidents in one day.

Ongoing Health Issues for Your Basset

Gastric Torsion (Bloat)

Gastric torsion, or bloat, is a very serious health problem for all deep-chested breeds, of which the Basset is one. Bloat can painfully take the life of an otherwise perfectly healthy dog within just a few hours. This condition involves a swelling and twisting (torsion) of the dog's stomach from water, gas, or both.

Just why bloat occurs is still relatively unknown. There are many suggested causes, but most experts believe that bloat may occur when conditions are just right and one or more suggested causes are present. Some of these causes are thought to be:

• A large meal, particularly of dry dog food, followed by a large intake of water, followed by strenuous exercise.

• A genetic predisposition in some breeds (the Basset's close kin, the Bloodhound, is one of these) and even in some lineages within breeds.

• Stress from one of many sources, like a severe electrical storm, for example.

• The age of the dog. Being more than 24 months old increases the possibility of bloat.

• The sex of the dog. Males seem to bloat more often than females.

A two-year-old male Basset from a family that has had several other members die of gastric torsion would seem to be a definite candidate for this condition. The clinical signs of gastric torsion are:

1. Obvious abdominal pain and noticeable swelling of the abdomen.

2. Excessive salivation and very rapid breathing.

3. Pale, cool-to-the-touch skin on the gum and in the mouth.

4. A dazed and shocked look.

5. Repeated attempts by the dog to vomit but with nothing coming up.

Bloat is a true emergency. Alert your veterinarian and then immediately transport your Basset to the clinic.

Canine Hip Dysplasia (CHD)

Canine hip dysplasia is among one of the most discussed subjects in the purebred dog world. CHD is a medical condition in which the hip joint is slack, or loose. This looseness is combined with a deformity of the socket of the hip and the ball-like femoral head joining the thighbone. This defective development of the hip and its connective tissues produces an unstable hip joint that results in a wobbly gait that clearly hurts the dog.

CHD is not always clearly caused by inheritable factors, but a smart Basset buyer will try to obtain a puppy from parentage that is free of this disorder. The Orthopedic Foundation for Animals (OFA) has developed a widely-used X-ray process that can often detect the presence of CHD. This test is best used in dogs over the age of two years. A new test, considered by many to be an improvement over OFA's X-rays is the Penn-Hip test, which needs a specially trained veterinarian to conduct it.

Giving Your Dog Medicine

One way to give your dog pills is to hide the medicine inside some treat. A more direct method is to open the Basset's mouth, tilt its throat back just a little, placing the pill as far back on the dog's tongue as possible. Close the dog's mouth and wait for him to swallow.

Never throw a pill into a dog's mouth or tilt his head way back. This could result in the pill going into the dog's windpipe instead of down its throat. Give liquid medicine in much the same manner, never tilting the head back very far. Simply pour the liquid medicine into the "pocket" formed by the corner of the dog's mouth. You can then tilt the head back just a small amount as you hold the mouth shut and rub the underside of the dog's throat until you are sure that it has swallowed the medicine.

Another hint about medicines: Don't give a dog human medicine and always implicitly follow your veterinarian's instruction of how much of a medication to give your dog and when. Always continue giving the medicine until you have administered all of it.

Living a Good Long Life

If you have taken good care of your Basset, fed correctly, provided enough exercise, taken him to the veterinarian on a regular basis, then you can expect that your long and short companion can have a long and happy life and be with you for 12 or more years.

Euthanasia

One day you will see your aged Basset Hound in a new way. The oldster has been a faithful companion. He may have helped rear your children. You have probably walked thousands of miles together during your daily strolls over the

This old Basset Hound has lived a long and enjoyable life. When life no longer is enjoyable, responsible dog owners and their veterinarians have a difficult, but necessary choice to make.

years. You love the old dog and you know that it loves you. Then something changes.

There will come a day when your old Basset can't move very well anymore. He will be in pain much of the time and will glance at you with those pleading, sad eyes asking you to make the pain go away, to make things be as they once were.

Because you can't turn back the calendar to a time when life was better and less hurtful for your old friend, you must face the most painful choice a dog owner must ever have to face. When is enough? When do you steel yourself to say good-bye to your old Basset, not for your sake but for his sake?

Your veterinarian can help you know the right time, but only you can make the terrible choice between bad and worse, between keeping this old treasure with you even though his life is filled with pain, and letting the old dog go, marking an end to his suffering. Only you can know when to say good-bye.

Organizations

American Kennel Club
51 Madison Avenue
New York, NY 10038
(212) 696-8200

AKC Registration and Information
5580 Centerview Drive, Suite 200
Raleigh, NC 27606-3390
(919) 233-9767

Bobbi Brandt
Basset Hound Club of America
11401 Gamache Drive
Anchorage, AK 99516

Canadian Kennel Club
89 Skyway Avenue
Etobicoke, Ontario
Canada M9W 6R4

American Boarding Kennel Association
4575 Galley Road, Suite 440A
Colorado Springs, CO 80915

Orthopedic Foundation for Animals
2300 Nifong Boulevard
Columbia, MO 651201
(314) 442-0418

Books

Alderton, David. *The Dog Care Manual.* Hauppauge, New York: Barron's Educational Series, Inc., 1986.

Baer, Ted. *Communicating With Your Dog.* Hauppauge, New York: Barron's Educational Series, Inc., 1989.

Walton, Margaret S. *The New Basset Hound.* New York, New York: Howell Book House, 1993.

About the Author

Joe Stahlkuppe is a widely read magazine and newspaper pet columnist, author, pet radio host, and freelance feature writer. An acknowledged pet expert, he has written over a dozen books for Barron's. An ordained pastor, Joe is a lifetime member of the Disabled American Veterans (DAV) and Vietnam Veterans of America, where he serves as a volunteer chaplain. He lives near Birmingham, Alabama, with his wife of many years, Cathie.

Acknowledgments

I am greatly indebted to the many volunteers who make up the Basset rescue organizations throughout the United States. These selfless individuals do what they do because they love Bassets and want to find them the best possible homes. Along with animal shelters, rescue organizations fill a crucial void for Basset Hounds (and all other breeds of dog).

I would especially like to acknowledge Basset Hound Rescue of Alabama and to single out Bob "Stretch" and Eunice Cleeland for the valuable work that they do.

This book is further dedicated to a great dog man, my late uncle Frank Stahlkuppe of Hiawassee, Georgia.

I also want to thank the editorial staff at Barron's Educational Series, Inc., for their tireless efforts to make this book an informative one.

Important Note

This pet owner's manual tells the reader how to buy or adopt and care for a Basset Hound. The author and publisher consider it important to point out that the advice given in this book is meant primarily for normally developed dogs of excellent physical health and good character.

Anyone who adopts a fully grown dog should be aware that the animal has already formed its basic impressions of humans. The new owner should watch the dog carefully, including its behavior toward humans, and should meet the previous owner.

Caution is further advised in the association of children with dogs, in meeting with other dogs, and in exercising the dog without proper safeguards.

Even well-behaved and carefully supervised dogs sometimes do damage to someone else's property or cause accidents. It is therefore in the owner's interest to be adequately insured against such eventualities, and we strongly urge all dog owners to purchase a liability policy that covers their dog(s).

Cover Photos

Front cover: Shutterstock; inside front cover: Isabelle Francais; inside back cover: Isabelle Francais; and back cover: Norvia Behling.

Photo Credits

Norvia Behling: 4, 7, 11, 12, 16, 22 (bottom), 26, 28, 31, 32, 33, 44, 45, 48, 54, 66, 67, 70, 71, 77, 79, 83, and 92; Isabelle Francais: 2-3, 5, 8, 13, 14, 15, 17, 19, 20, 21, 22 (left and top), 27, 30, 34, 35, 36, 39, 40, 41, 43, 45, 46, 50, 51, 55, 56, 57, 58, 59, 60, 62, 65, 68, 72, 75, 76, 79, 80, 81, and 93; Shutterstock: 18 and 72; and Connie Summers: 91.

© Copyright 2008, 1998 by Barron's Educational Series, Inc.

All inquiries should be addressed to:
Barron's Educational Series, Inc.
250 Wireless Boulevard
Hauppauge, NY 11788
www.barronseduc.com

ISBN-13: 978-0-7641-3774-7
ISBN-10: 0-7641-3774-3

Library of Congress Catalog Card No. 2007042364

Library of Congress Cataloging-in-Publication Data
Stahlkuppe, Joe.
    Basset hounds : everything about purchase, training, feeding, and health care / Joe Stahlkuppe; illustrations by Michele Earle-Bridges.
      p. cm.
    Includes index.
    ISBN-13: 978-0-7641-3774-7 (alk. paper)
    ISBN-10: 0-7641-3774-3 (alk. paper)
    1. Basset hound. I. Title.

SF429.B2S74 2008
636.753'6—dc22   2007042364

Printed in China
9 8 7 6 5 4 3 2 1